HEINEMANN GEOGRAPHY

Series Editor: John Hopkin

Global SUPERPOWERS

MEL ROCKETT CELIA TIDMARSH

HEINEMANN EDUCATIONAL

Heinemann Educational
a division of Heinemann Educational Books Ltd.
Halley Court, Jordan Hill, Oxford OX2 8EJ

OXFORD LONDON EDINBURGH
MADRID ATHENS BOLOGNA PARIS
MELBOURNE SYDNEY AUCKLAND SINGAPORE
TOKYO IBADAN NAIROBI HARARE
GABORONE PORTSMOUTH NH (USA)

First published 1992

A catalogue record for this book is available from the British Library

ISBN 0 435 35192 3

Designed and produced by Gecko Limited, Bicester, Oxon

Printed and bound in Spain by Mateu Cromo

Notes to teachers

Details of National Curriculum Statements of Attainment covered are given on the pupil spreads; italics indicate partial coverage. A summary of the Statements of Attainment coverage is given in the matrix in the accompanying Teacher's Resource Pack.

Acknowledgements

The Publishers would like to thank the following for permission to reproduce photographs:

Ace Photo Agency, pp. 5(K), 13(D, G), 16(C) (Mugshots), 16(E) (Gabe Palmer), 18(D) (Benelux Press); Art Directors, p. 16(B); Aspect Picture Library, pp. 4(E), 8(A, C), 16(A) (Vince Streano), 16(D) (Peter Chinnery), 28(G), 29(H), 41(E, F), 47(E); Barnaby's Picture Library, p. 4(F); J. Allan Cash Ltd, pp. 4(D), 8(B), 10(A), 13(H), 21(F), 24(A), 28(E), 29(I), 34(B); Thomas Clay, p. 4(B); Greg Evans Photo Library, pp. 17(F), 34(A); Gamma/Frank Spooner, p. 20(A); Robert Harding Picture Library, pp. 5(L), 7(G, J), 9(G, F), 11(E), 22(top left), 26(D), 39(C); Harrison–Church, p. 5(I); John Hillelson © Howard Sochurer, p. 10(C); Holt, p. 23(middle right); Hutchison Library, p. 28(D); Image Bank, pp. 4(C), 6(D, E), 22(bottom left), 23(top right), 42(C), 46(C); Magnum, pp. 19(E), 45(E), 46(B), 47(D); Nippon Steel, pp. 29(K), 30(C), 31(E) (Mike O'Neill); Novosti Press Agency, pp. 9(E); Panos Pictures, pp. 7(H), 22(bottom right); Picturepoint, pp. 29(J), 32(B); Andrej Reiser/Bilderberg, p. 37(E); SCR Library, pp. 36(C), 37(F); Frank Spooner/P. Quittard, p. 37(D); TCL Stock Directory, pp. 19(G), 21(G); Topham/Associated Press, pp. 19(F), 43(E); USSR Photo Library, pp. 5(H), 43(D).

Cover photographs by J. Allan Cash Ltd (Tokyo at night) and Sally and Richard Greenhill (crowd of people).

Thanks are also due to the following for permission to reproduce copyright material: From Michael Fidron and Ronald Segal, *The New State of the World Atlas*, 3rd. ed., London/New York, 1987, p.9(D); Foreign Press Center/Japan, *Facts and Figures of Japan 1989*, pp. 24(B,C), 25(F), 26(B, C), 27(E, F), 28(A, C, F); *Geography*, Vol. 73, October 1988, by John Sargent, published by The Geographical Association, p. 30(A); Government of Japan, Environment Agency, p.33(D); International Society for Educational Information, *Supply and Demand for Energy in Japan*, pp. 24(B), 25(E); Ministry of Supply and Services, Canada, *US-Canada MOI*, Work Group 1, 1981, p. 21(D); Mobil Corporation, *Mobil Factbook*, 1990, p. 18(C); Thomas Nelson and Sons Ltd, *The Active World* by P. Jones and B. Pike, p. 32(A); George Philip Limited, *New Philip's Modern School Atlas*, pp. 25(D), 41(G, H); RIA-Novosti (London), *USSR Yearbook, 1988*, p. 39 (D, E); Courtesy of Shell Briefing Service, pp. 18(B), 36(A, B).

The Publishers have made every effort to trace copyright holders. However, if any material has been incorrectly acknowledged, we would be pleased to correct this at the earliest opportunity.

Contents

Contrasting landscapes

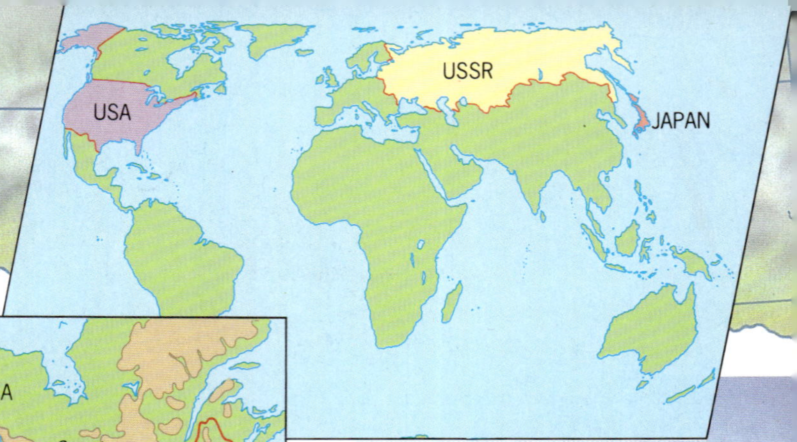

A Physical features, USA

B Yosemite National Park, California

C Mendenhall Glacier, Alaska

D Prairies and cattle, Nebraska

E Skiing

F Japanese jungle, Kyushu

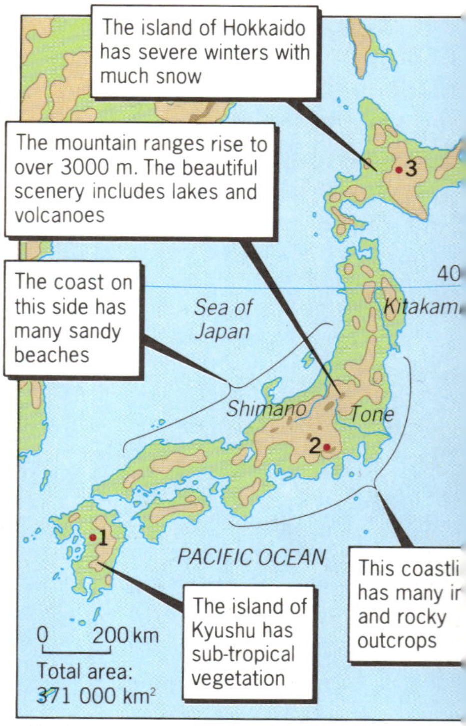

G Physical features, Japan

H ***The Taiga, Yakutia, Siberia***

I ***Karakum Desert, Turkmenistan***

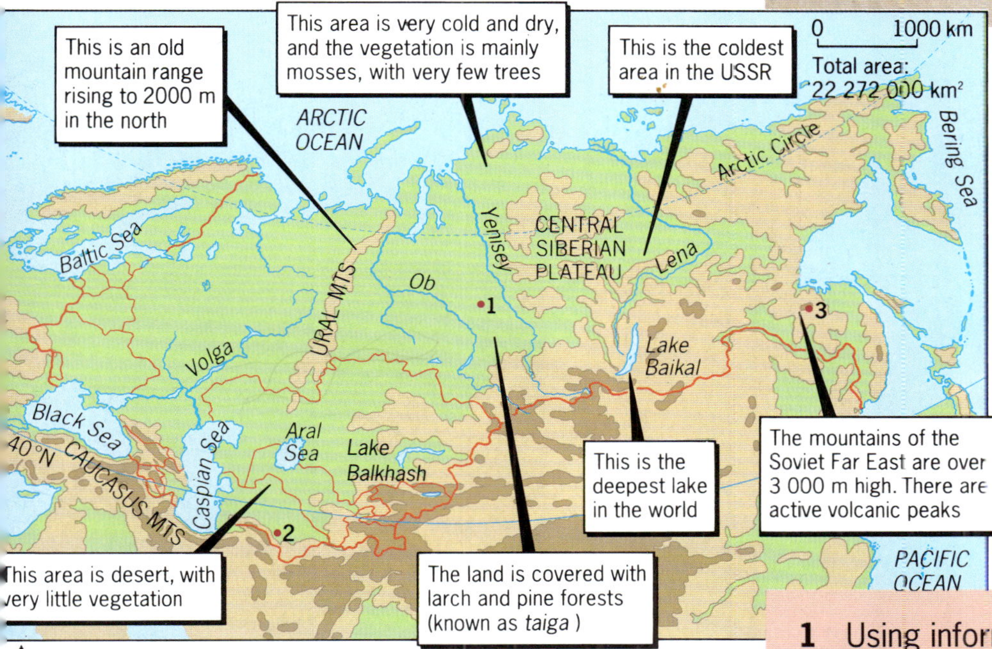

J ***Physical features, USSR***

K ***The Soviet Far East mountains***

L ***Mount Fuji, Honshu***

1 Using information from A, G and J, and from an atlas, match up the photos with the locations shown on each map.

2 Use the maps and photos from these pages plus an atlas to complete a copy of the table below:

	USA	USSR	Japan
Mountains			
Rivers			
Main climates			
Main vegetation types			
Other features, e.g. plains, lakes, etc.			

People of the superpowers

A ***The growth of populations***

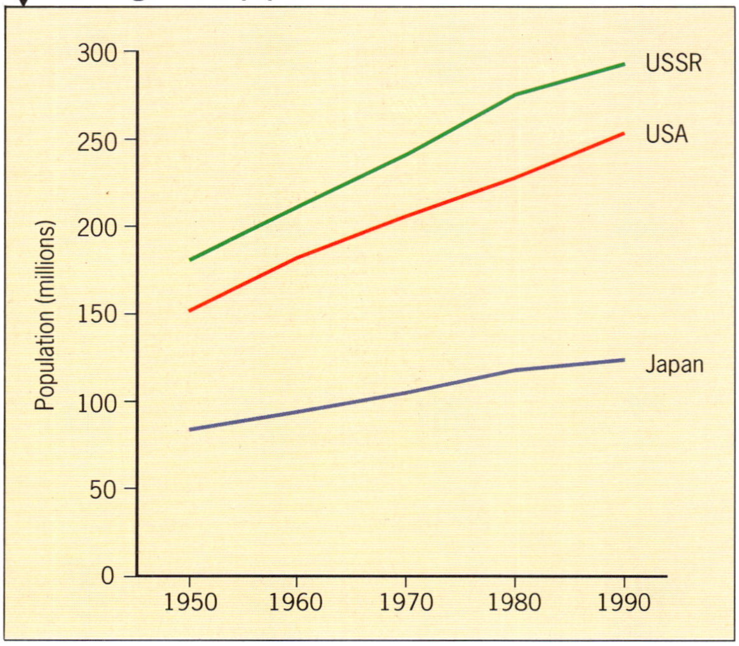

	USA	USSR	Japan
1950	64	40	38
1970	74	55	68
1990	74	66	77

B ***The move to the cities (% of urban population)***

The former USSR has the third highest population in the world. The population is made up of about 100 separate national groups. e.g. Armenians, Russians and Kazaks. These groups are mostly based in the different **republics** of the USSR.

D ***A Soviet family***

C ***Where people live in the USSR***

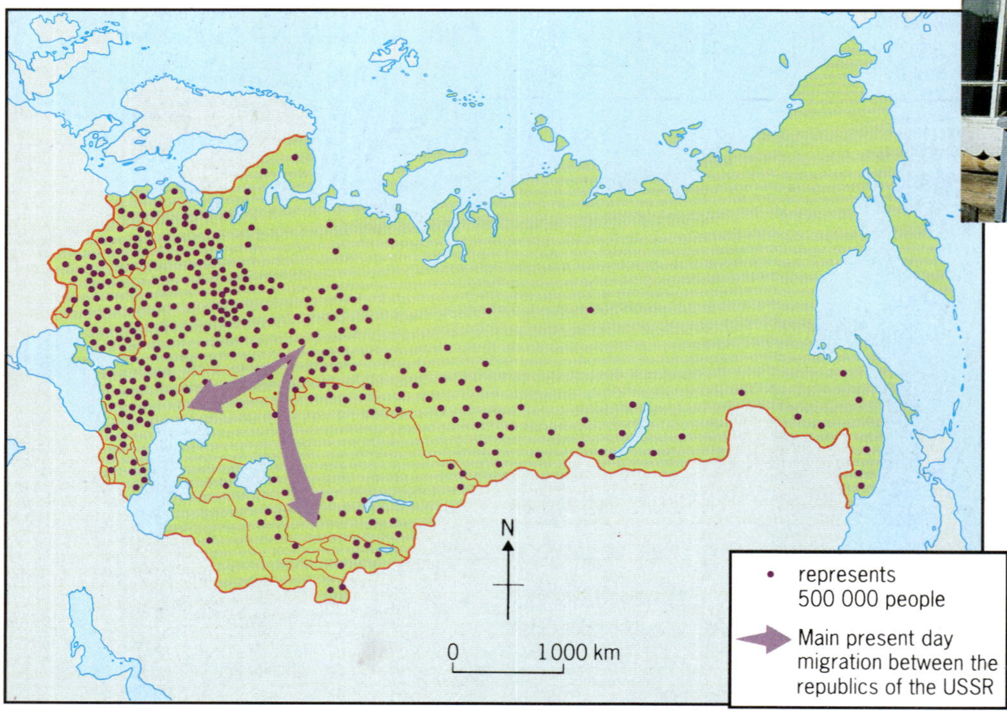

E ***Samarkand Market, USSR***

The USA has the fourth highest population in the world. Since the early 19th century many people have moved to the USA from other countries. This means an extremely varied population today.

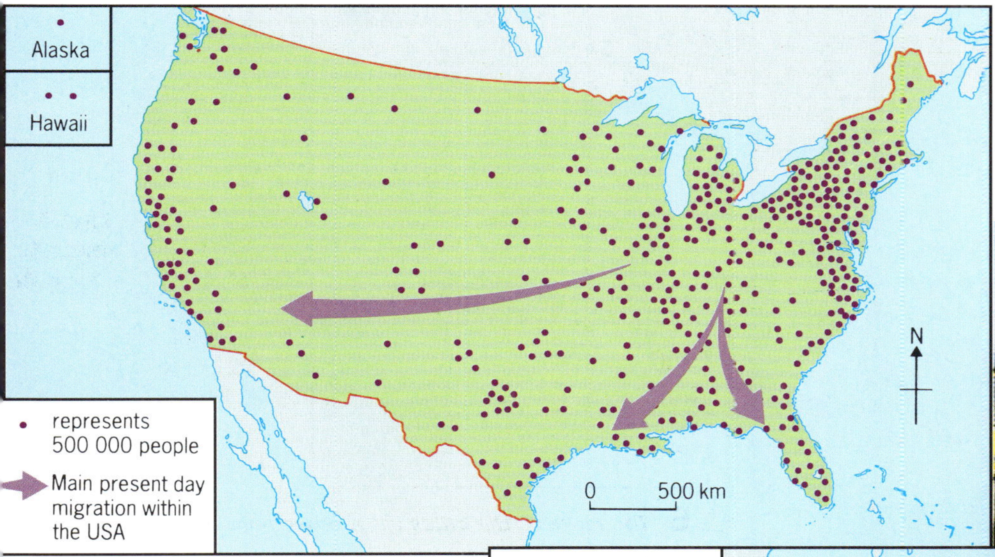

F ***Where people live in the USA***

G ***Schoolchildren, USA***

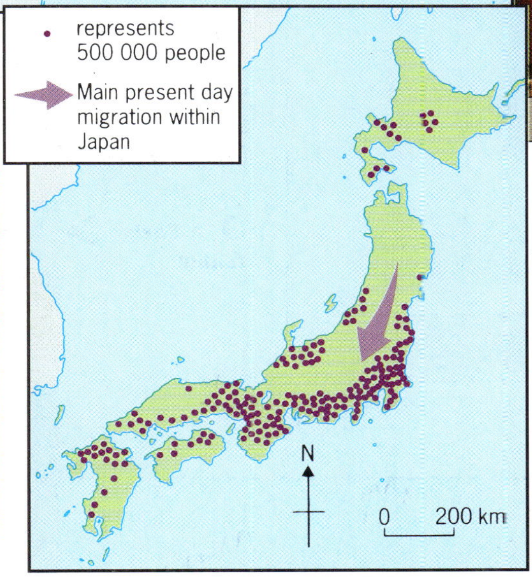

I ***Where people live in Japan***

H ***Coney Island, New York***

J ***Crowds in Shibuya, Japan***

Japan has the seventh highest population in the world. It is also one of the most densely populated countries. **Migration** into or out of Japan has never been very high and has had little effect on the population.

1. Study graph A.
   - **a** Give figures to illustrate what happened to the total population of each country between 1950 and 1990.
   - **b** What are the main differences?
2. Using information from B, C, F and I, write an account of the migration taking place in each country.
3. Study maps C, F and I and, using information from pages 4 and 5 and an atlas, suggest reasons why people choose to live in some places rather than others.

Superpowers at work

Japan, the USA and the former USSR are industrial **superpowers**. Between them they dominate world production of food, **minerals**, **energy** and **manufactured goods**. The USA and USSR are two of the world's largest countries and possess huge **reserves** of **natural resources**. Japan, however, has relatively few resources and yet has become the second most important exporter of manufactured goods in the world.

C *Unloading cotton, Uzbekhistan*

A *Wheat harvest, USA*

B *Cattle farm, USA*

USA
World's leading agricultural producer
15% of world food exports
Highly mechanized farming
Rich in mineral resources
Leading manufacturing nation
Hi-tech computers etc. – California
Petro-chemicals – Texas
Engineering and metals – North East

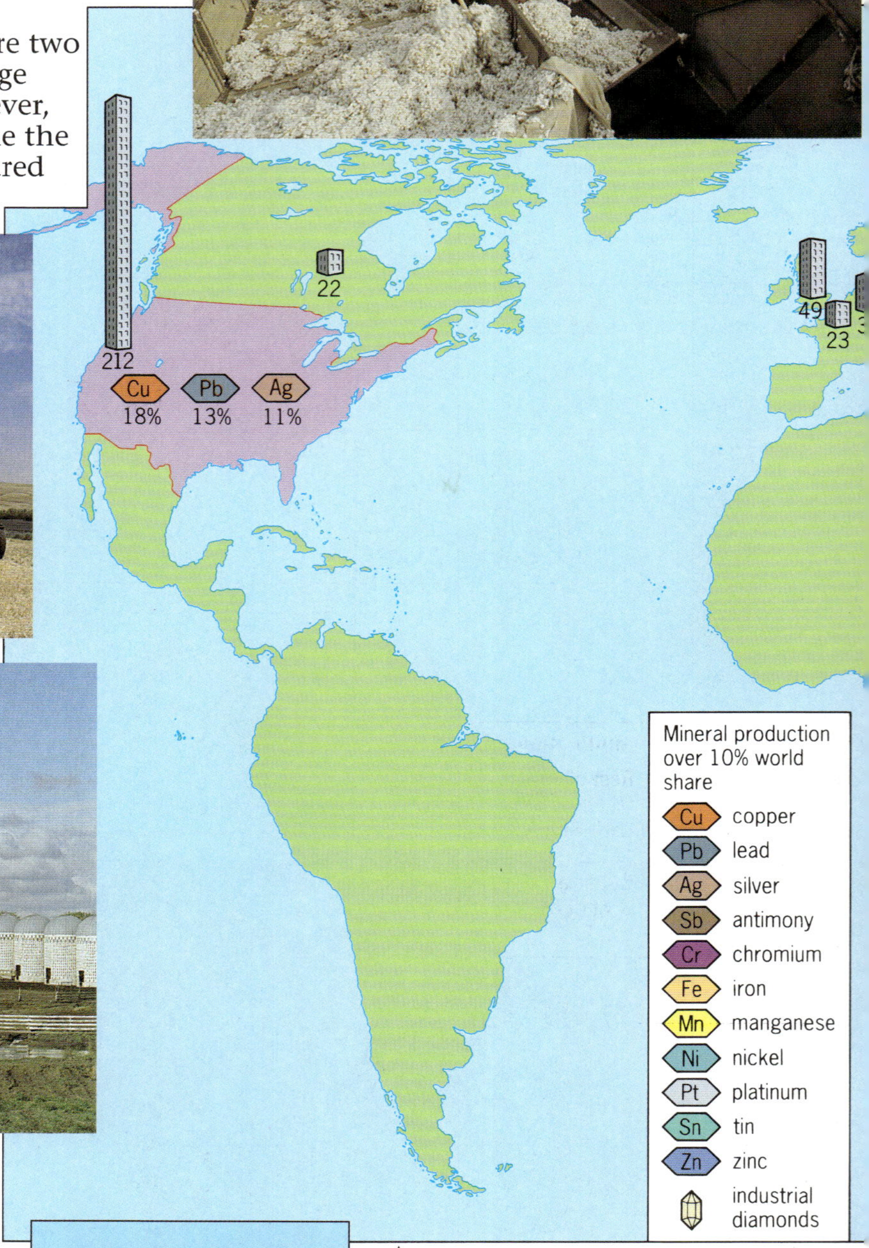

GDP per capita (1988)

USA	$18 448
USSR	$3518
Japan	$19 464

D *Mineral resources in the superpowers*

USSR
Modernized industry after 1917 revolution
Large-scale **heavy industry**
Great mineral wealth
50% world iron-ore reserves
30% world industrial diamonds
'Extensive' agriculture

E *Kirov factory*

Japan
Few natural resources
'Intensive' farming
Raw materials and food imported
Second largest manufacturing nation

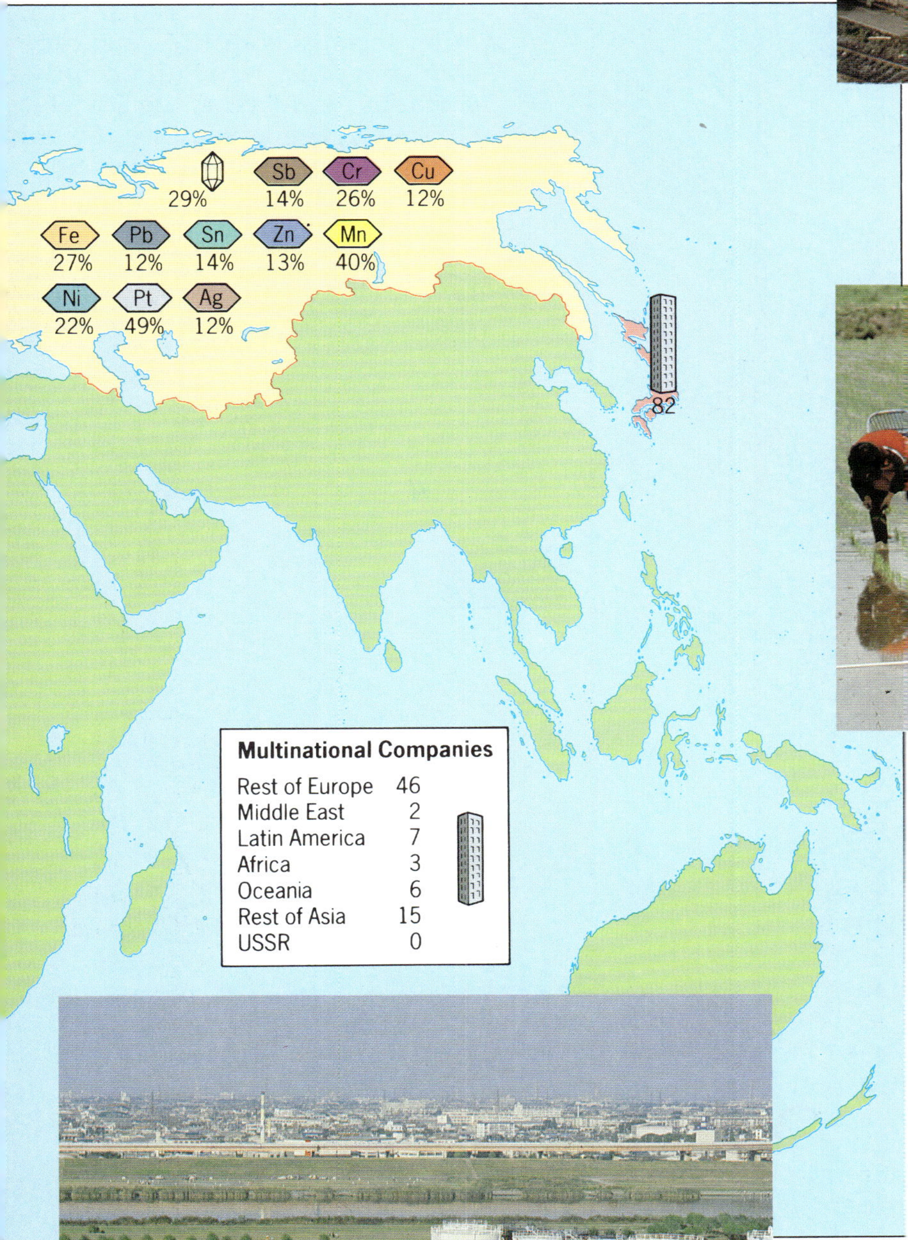

Multinational Companies

Rest of Europe	46
Middle East	2
Latin America	7
Africa	3
Oceania	6
Rest of Asia	15
USSR	0

F *Planting rice, Japan*

1 a Use the materials on these pages to compare the mineral wealth of the three superpowers. You could do this by drawing a table using the figures on the map.
b Which country has the greatest mineral wealth?
c Is this the most successful country in terms of industrial power? (Use the **GDP** figures in the box at the base of the map.)

G *Industry, Tokyo Bay*

International trade

A *Aircraft made in the US aerospace industry*

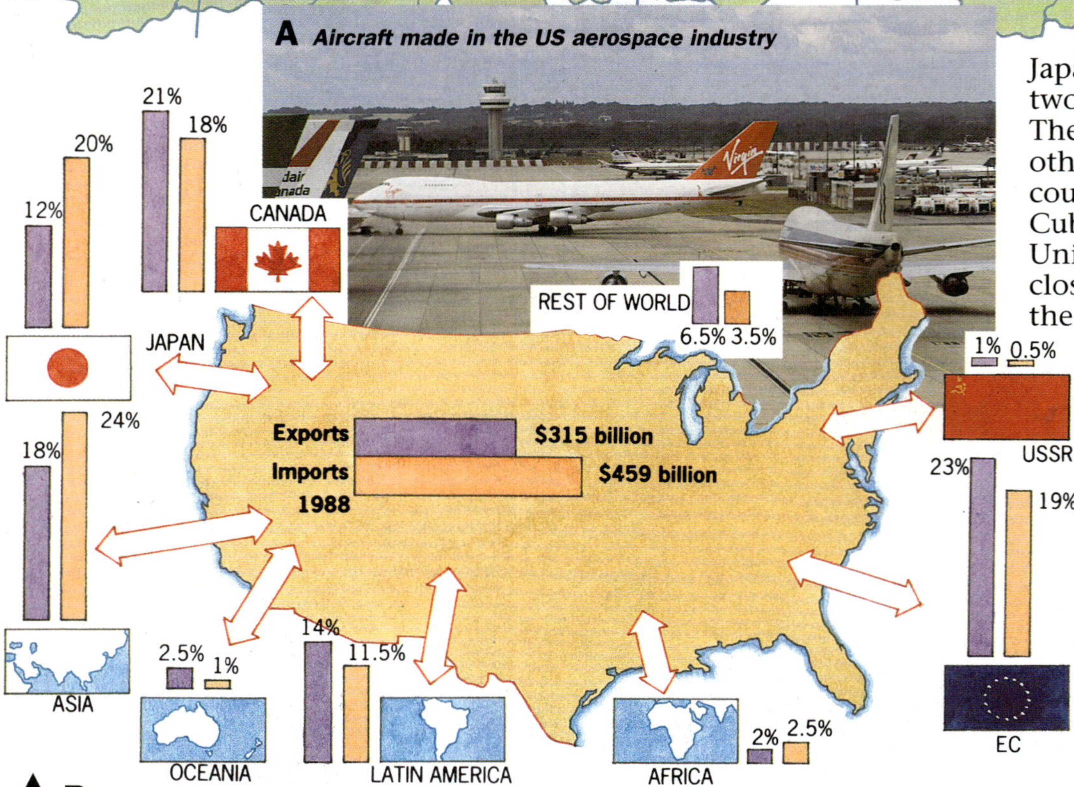

B *USA: exports and imports*

Japan and the USA are the world's two greatest **trading nations**. The former USSR has traded with other socialist countries, e.g. the countries of Eastern Europe and Cuba. In recent years the Soviet Union has begun to move towards closer trading relationships with the rest of the world.

C *Siberian pipeline*

Free trade or protection?

Japan and the USA manufacture cars. Japan sells large numbers of cars in the USA. US companies have lost sales and closed down several factories. Thousands of jobs have been lost. Some Americans think that Japanese cars should be banned. This is called **protection**. If all countries banned the products of their rivals there would be less trade, lower sales and fewer jobs.

The alternative to protection is **free trade** with no **import duties** or **barriers**. This system is said to provide plentiful supplies of cheap goods.

International trade today is a mixture of protection and free trade. Rich countries profit most from this. They buy food and raw materials from poor countries at low prices. Their manufactured goods are then sold for large profits. Poor countries find it difficult to set up manufacturing because they lack **capital**. If they do manage to establish industries they find that rich countries protect their own firms by imposing import duties and **quotas** on these goods.

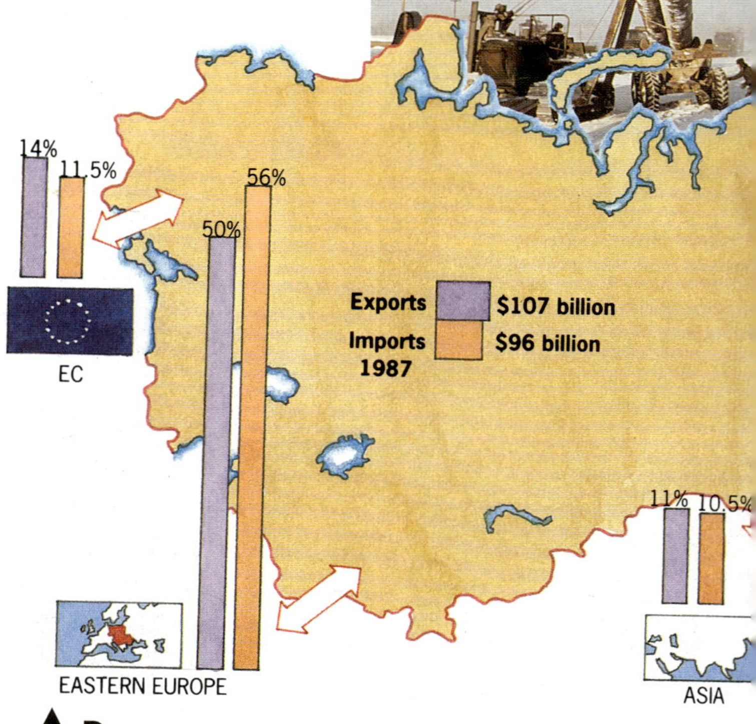

D *USSR: exports and imports*

E ***Container ship, Yokohama harbour***

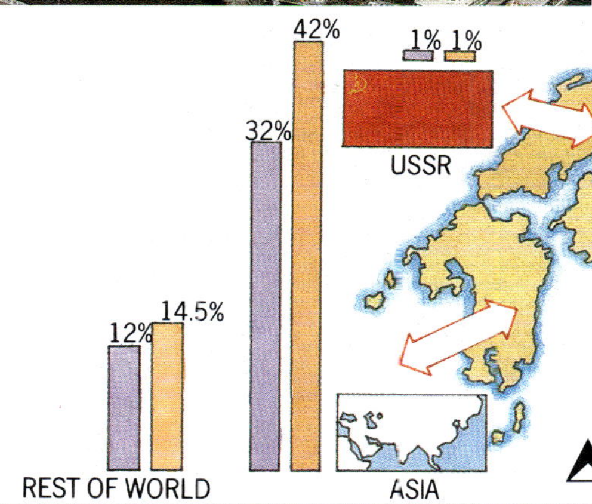
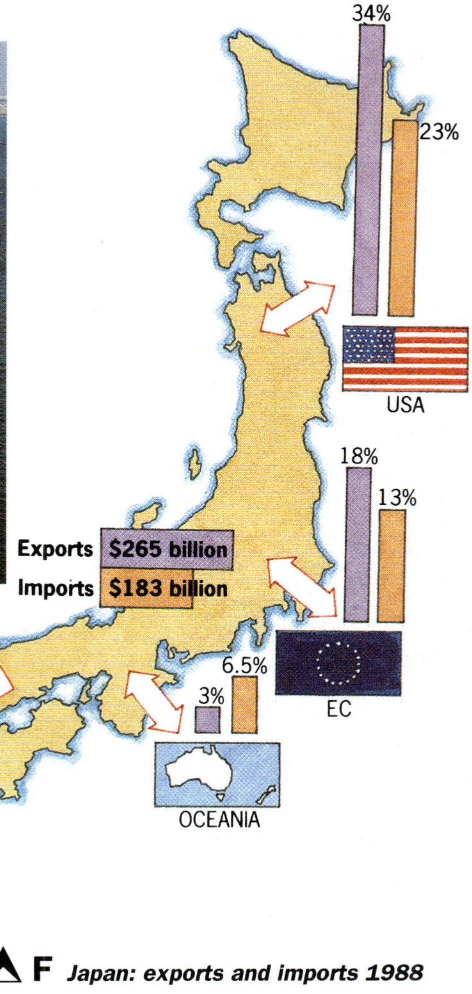

▲ F ***Japan: exports and imports 1988***

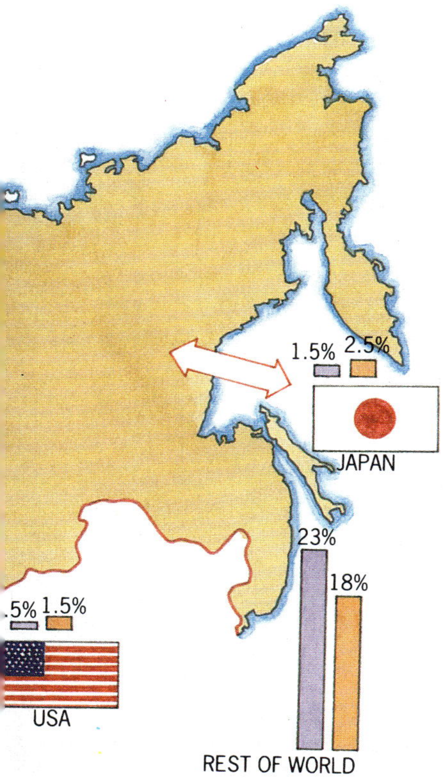

1 Study the three photographs on these pages. What do they tell you about the types of goods made and exported by the three economic superpowers? What might be in the containers being exported from Japan?

2 Compare the total imports and exports for each of the three countries shown on the maps. Put them in rank order – biggest first. Why do you think the USSR, which has vast mineral and energy resources, is so much less important as a trading nation than the other two countries?

3 If the USSR develops its industry in the same way that Japan and the USA have, how might this affect the trade of other manufacturing countries?

4 Make a collection of advertisements for electrical and electronic goods, motor vehicles etc. which have been made in the USA, Japan or the USSR. These adverts could be mounted as a collage. Which country seems to sell the most goods in the UK?

Energy in the USA

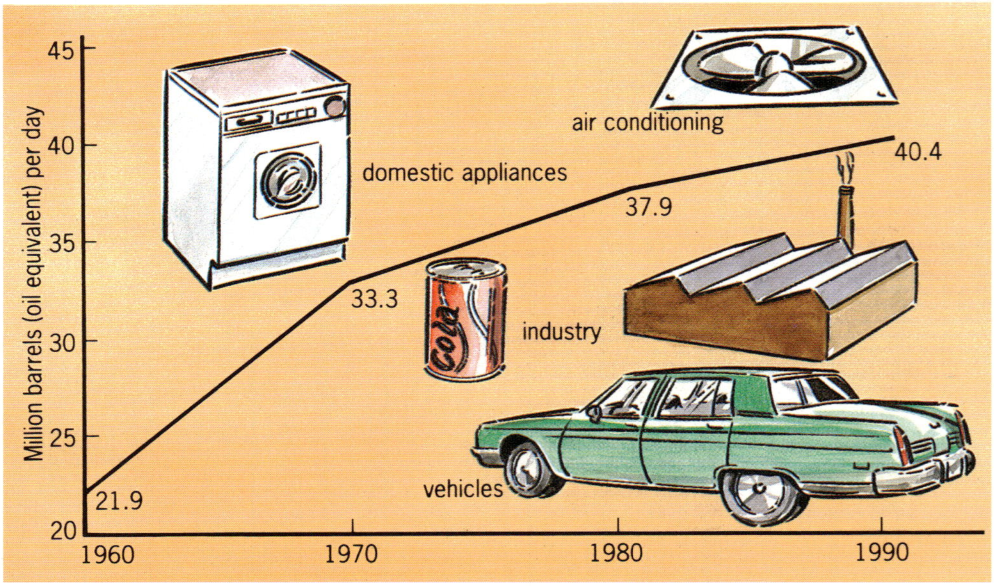

A ***Energy consumption in the USA***

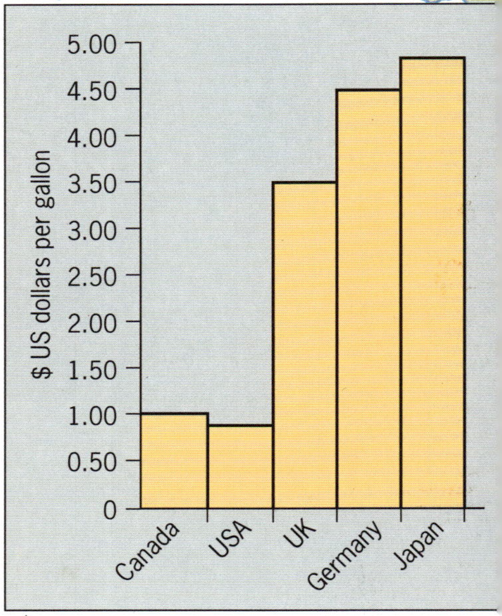

B ***The price of petrol***

People in the USA use more energy per person than any other country. They use it to keep warm in winter and cool in summer. They use large amounts of cheap petrol in their cars. Their domestic appliances – fridges, TVs, dishwashers etc. – and industries consume a great deal of energy.

North America has large reserves of **fossil fuels** – coal, oil and gas – but these are becoming more expensive to find and extract, e.g. in Alaska and the Gulf of Mexico. **Oil shale** and coal are extracted by **strip mining** which scars the landscape. Burning the coal in power stations causes **acid rain**. Plans to produce 20 per cent of US energy through **nuclear power** have been shelved since the disasters at Three Mile Island (1976) in the USA and Chernobyl (1986) in the former USSR.

Americans are trying to supply more of their energy needs with cleaner, renewable sources of power such as **solar power**, wind power and **hydro-electricity**.

C ***Why worry?***

D ***Hi-tech windmills on a Californian hillside***

G ***The Trans-Alaska pipeline***

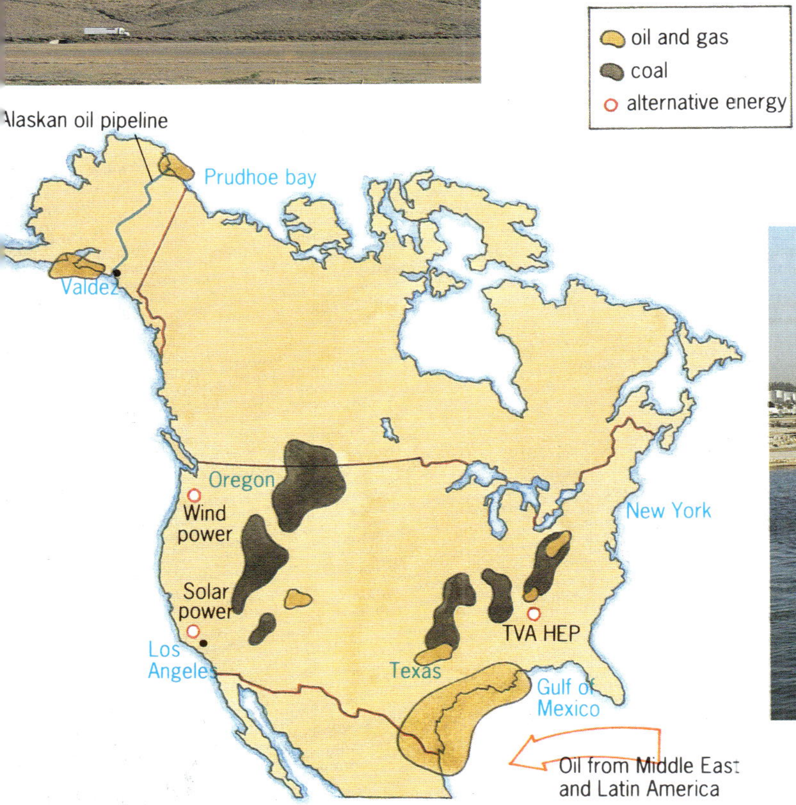

H ***Oil tankers unloading in Florida***

E ***Sources of energy in the USA***

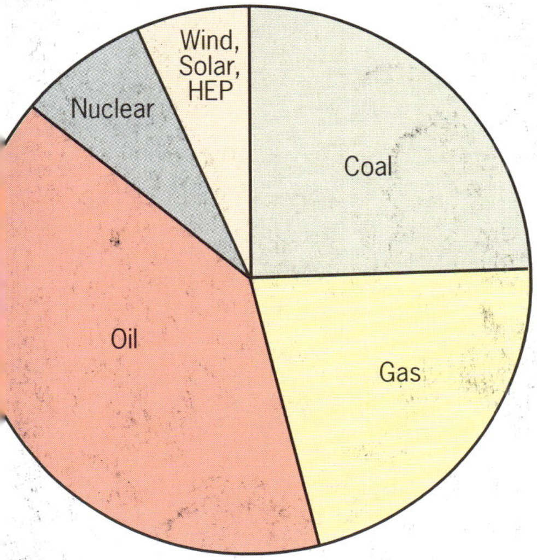

F ***Energy consumption in the USA, by source***

1. Why do Americans consume so much energy:
   a per person?
   b in total?
2. Which other countries would you expect to be major consumers of energy? Why?
3. Americans are worried about petrol supplies because they rely so much upon their cars. Petrol is cheaper in the USA than in any other developed country. Would it help to save fuel if the US government raised petrol prices by adding more tax on petrol sales?

   In your group you might debate a proposal to raise petrol prices in the USA. Consider the likely points of view of these people: car owners, environmentalists, politicians, factory owners, petrol companies, consumers of other goods.

Gg 2/6e, 7e; Gg 5/5b, 6a

Made in the USA

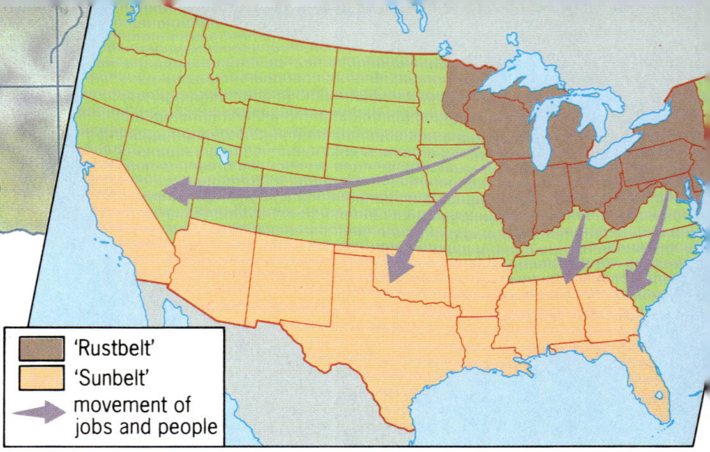

In the North East of the USA is one of the world's major manufacturing areas, the 'Manufacturing Belt', or 'Rustbelt' as it has become known. This traditional heartland of American industry was based on the making of iron and steel, and steel products such as ships, motor vehicles and machinery.

These industries used iron ore from the Great Lakes orefields and coal from the Appalachian mountains. As the cities of the area grew, so did the pool of **semi-skilled** and **skilled** workers and the size of the local **market** for the goods they made.

This area has seen a major decline in manufacturing and employment since the 1960s.

A ***The Rustbelt***

B *The Sunbelt*

America's new industries are based on **electronics**, **information systems**, aerospace engineering, plastics and chemicals. Most of these don't need to be close to raw materials, fuel supplies or a large pool of labour. Their products are relatively light and can be transported easily to markets anywhere in the USA or the rest of the world. These factories are **footloose**. They can be located almost anywhere. The main needs are for a well-educated workforce, plenty of capital to invest in new buildings and machinery, a suitable site, attractive environment and good communications.

Many new industries have been located in the 'Sunbelt' of southern and south western USA. Movement to California has slowed down as the Sunbelt has developed. 'Silicon valley' in California was the first centre of the new **'sunrise' industries**. This was the centre of microchip technology in the computer and aerospace industries.

1. On an outline map of the USA shade in the Rustbelt and the Sunbelt. Add to your map the major cities of these two regions. You will need to use an atlas. Only include cities with over one million inhabitants.
2. Write a paragraph about each of the two areas explaining why people and industries have left the North East of the USA and moved to the South.

Petro-chemicals in the USA

What are petro-chemicals?

A The USA is sometimes known as the country of the motor car. Huge amounts of oil are used to manufacture petrol and diesel fuel to keep America on the move.

B Plastic film and packaging are made from oil-based chemicals. Paper is treated with chemicals.

C Plastic is made from oil. Few parts of our lives are not affected by plastic products.

D Much of the food grown in the USA is produced with the aid of chemical fertilizers.

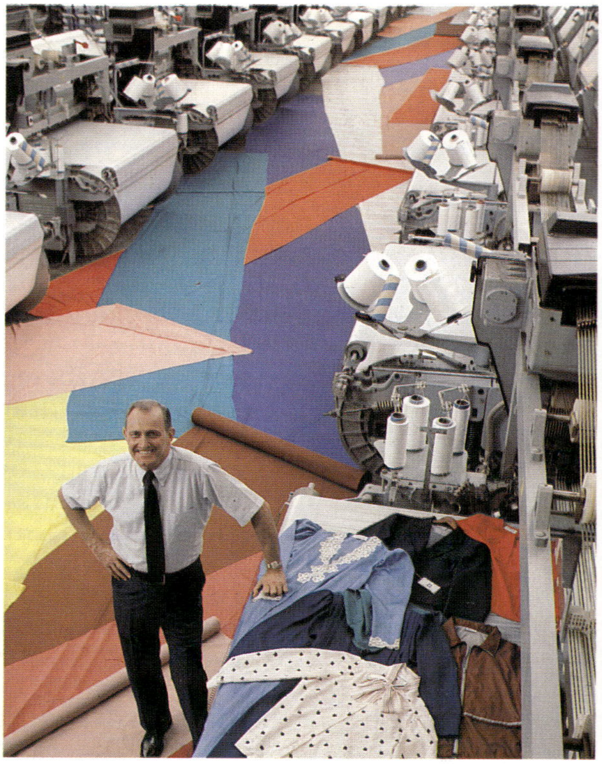

E Oil is used to make **synthetic** textiles. Americans wearing nylon, acrylic or polyester are wearing oil products.

The petro-chemical industry also produces detergents, paints, cosmetics and **pharmaceuticals**.

How are they made?

Petro-chemical **refineries** are found all over the USA, especially in the South and California. These refineries are huge industrial plants.

A suitable location for a refinery has to satisfy several requirements:

1 Raw materials

Petro-chemicals are made from oil. California produces oil and is well placed to receive supplies from Alaska.

2 Energy

A refinery uses large amounts of electricity - as much as many towns.

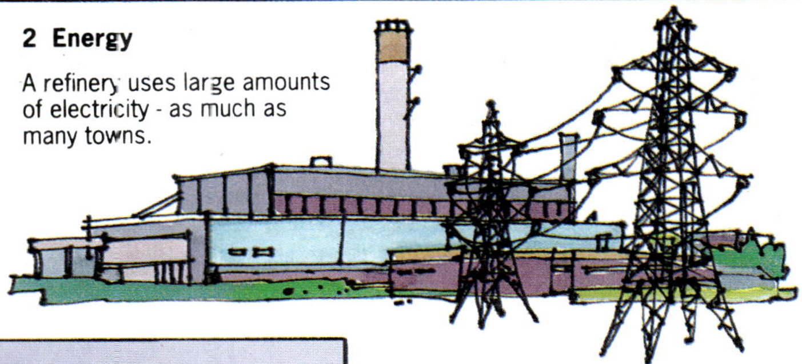

F ***Petro-chemical factory at night***

3 Capital

Refineries cost millions of dollars. Chevron is a giant corporation.

Markets

: large and uent population of the A provides a profitable market chemical products.

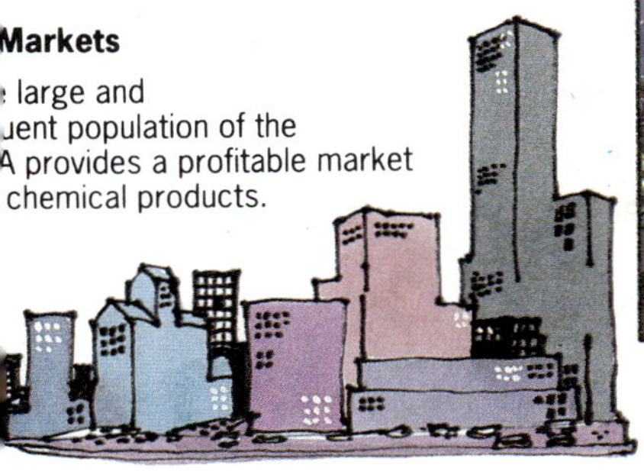

4 Workers

Refineries are automated but employ many skilled and unskilled workers.

5 Site

Refineries are large and need an extensive area of cheap, flat land.

6 Transport

Chemicals have to be delivered to customers by road, rail, sea or pipeline.

1 Using photo F draw a simple sketch of the petro-chemical works. Add labels to the sketch to explain the probable reasons for its location.

2 Petro-chemical works are usually located *either* close to a source of oil *or* close to a major market.
- **a** What would be the advantage of each of these two types of location?
- **b** What might be the disadvantages of each one?

3 At home investigate which goods are made from petro-chemical products.
- **a** Check the labels on clothing and note the synthetic materials used.
- **b** List ten products made from plastic.
- **c** List five items of packaging made from plastic or film.
- **d** Are any of these products labelled with the country of origin or the chemical they are made from?

Petro-chemicals – where to make them?

A ***The position of the Chevron chemical works in Richmond on the San Francisco Bay, California***

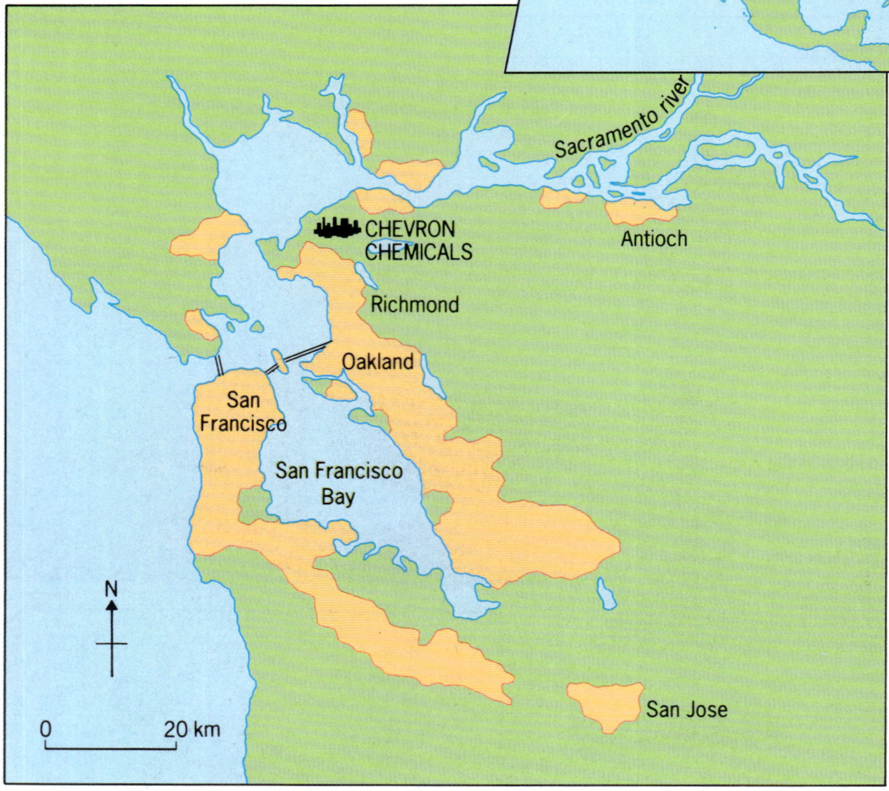

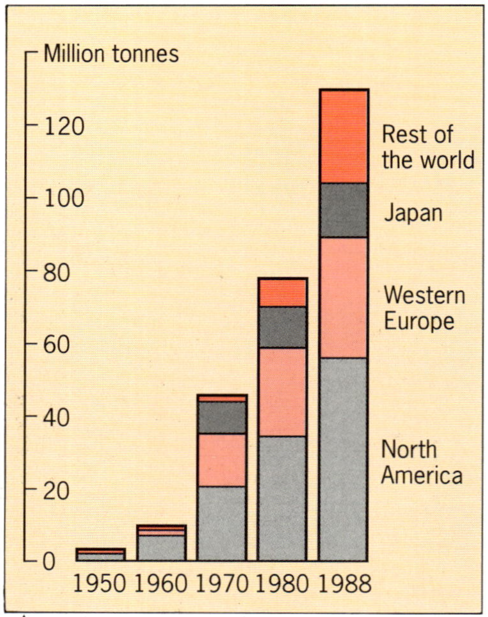

B ***Growth of the world's petro-chemical industry***

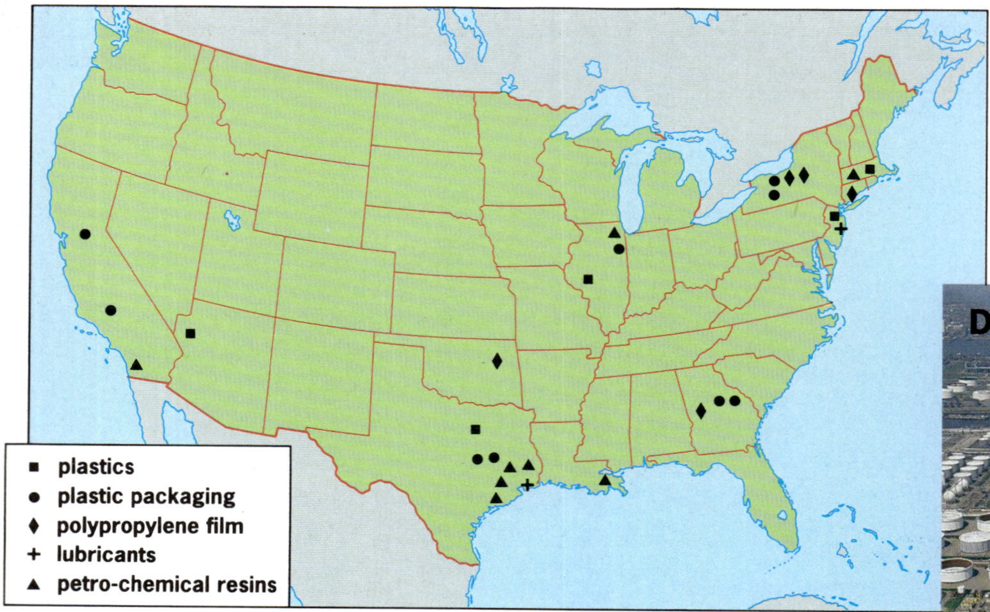

C ***The location of Mobil's chemical works in the USA***

Since the 1940s there has been a dramatic rise in the demand for petro-chemical products. The USA is the world's largest producer and consumer of these products.

Chevron and Mobil are just two of the many giant petro-chemical companies in the USA (see A and C).

D ***Petro-chemical refinery***

Environmental hazards

E ***Union Carbide disaster at Bhopal***

Chemicals are dangerous!

The leakage of poisonous chemical gas from the Union Carbide factory near Bhopal in India in 1984 killed thousands of local people and left more of them seriously ill. Union Carbide is a US multinational company.

An explosion at the Nypro chemical factory at Flixborough in Humberside in 1973 killed 28 workers and destroyed homes in the surrounding area. (Nypro is a subsidiary of a US company.)

Chemical products used by industry may leak into rivers and water supplies with devastating effects.

F ***Nypro disaster at Flixborough***

G ***A polluted river***

1 Look at map A. Draw a sketch map of the area. Use the information opposite and from an atlas to add these labels to your sketch. They show why Chevron located its refinery at Richmond.
- a flat site on the shores of San Francisco Bay
- money to build the works from Chevron
- plentiful supply of labour from Richmond
- large market in the San Francisco Bay areas
- imports of crude oil
- electricity from the Sacramento Valley (HEP)
- chemicals transported by rail, road and water

2 **a** What do you notice about the location of Mobil's refineries on map C?
b Can you identify five 'clusters' of refineries?
c Use an atlas map of the USA to suggest why the refineries are found in these areas.

3 If Chevron wanted to build a refinery in your area how would you react? Who might welcome such a plan? Who might object?

Environmental problems in the USA

A **Exxon Valdez** ***oil spill clean-up***

B ***The location of the*** **Exxon Valdez** ***oil spill in Prince William Sound, Alaska***

C ***Trying to put right the damage caused by the oil slick***

The Exxon Valdez disaster

24 March 1989. The **supertanker** *Exxon Valdez* ran aground in Prince William Sound, spilling thousands of tons of crude Alaskan oil into the bay. A massive oil slick spread southwards with the tide, contaminating many miles of shoreline. The fragile **ecosystem** of this cold temperate area is easily damaged and has a long recovery period. The shellfish and salmon fisheries were ruined and thousands of wild birds and mammals killed.

Exxon, one of the world's largest **multinational** companies, spent $1 billion on a clean-up campaign employing 11 000 workers. Only 20 per cent of the oil was collected. Nature was left to take care of the rest! US companies made large profits from this disaster by selling chemicals, equipment and labour for the campaign.

D ***Areas affected by acid rain in the USA***

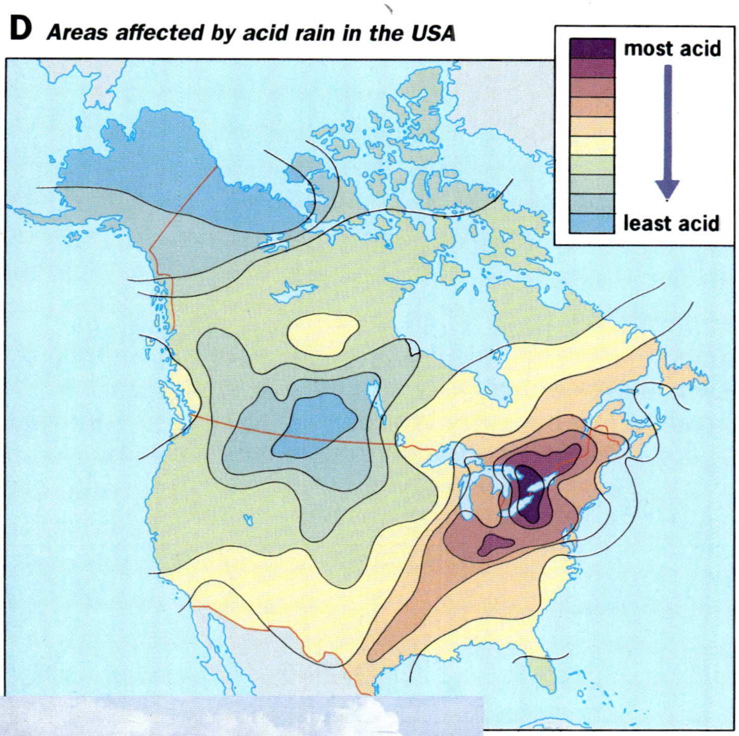

Dying Lakes in the Adirondacks

Acid rain from industrial North East of the USA has poisoned 90 per cent of the lakes in the Adirondack mountains.

Lake Erie Dies

Raw sewage has killed Lake Erie. Algae feeding on the sewage has smothered the lake, killing off its fishstocks.

POWER STATION POLLUTION

Each year 25 million tons of sulphur dioxide and 22 million tons of nitrous oxides are pumped into the atmosphere above the USA.

Chemical Time Bomb

The 'Valley of the Drums' in Kentucky contains 100 000 barrels of toxic chemical waste waiting to leak poisons into America's water supplies.

The Burning River

Oil and debris floating on the Cuyahoga river, Cleveland, erupted in flames to send a sheet of flames through the city.

POISONED SHELLFISH

20 per cent of US shellfish grounds have been poisoned by raw sewage.

E ***Newspaper headlines***

F ***Steel mill smokestacks in Pittsburgh, Pennsylvania***

Industrial acid rain **G**

Polluted USA

A growing population and industrial development threaten America's countryside. Until recently many Americans cared more about profit than about their environment. Power stations, steel and chemical works all pour **pollutants** into the air and water. Mining, quarrying and the timber industry create huge scars in the landscape.

Recently, environmental pressure groups have influenced public opinion and government decisions so that the rate of increase in pollution has slowed down. It still hasn't started to decrease!

1 Is it worth it? Oil extraction in sensitive environments such as Alaska can cause tremendous damage to the ecosystem. How can such damage be avoided? In your group discuss whether or not we should allow oil exploration and development in areas such as Alaska, Antarctica and Siberia.

2 Look at the headlines about pollution in the USA. Plot any places mentioned on a map of the USA. Use symbols to represent the types of pollution. Most power stations are found in the North East; the shellfish grounds affected are also in the North East and along the coast of California.

3 Draw a simple sketch map of Prince William Sound. Annotate your map with labels to show:

a the cause of the oil spillage
b the main effects of the pollution
c the measures taken to clean up the oil slick.

4 Investigate other major oil spillages, e.g. the Gulf War oil slick in the Persian Gulf, 1991; the *Amoco Cadiz* spillage off the French coast, 1978.

Gg 1/4f; Gg 2/7e; Gg 5/5a, 6a, 7a, 7c, 8b, 9a

USA: one nation – or many?

The USA is a huge country with over 246 million people. It is the world's richest country but not every part of the country, or every person, shares this wealth. The minority groups tend to be worst off, that is Black people descended from slaves, Hispanic (Spanish speaking) people from Mexico and Latin America, Asians and the surviving Native Americans.

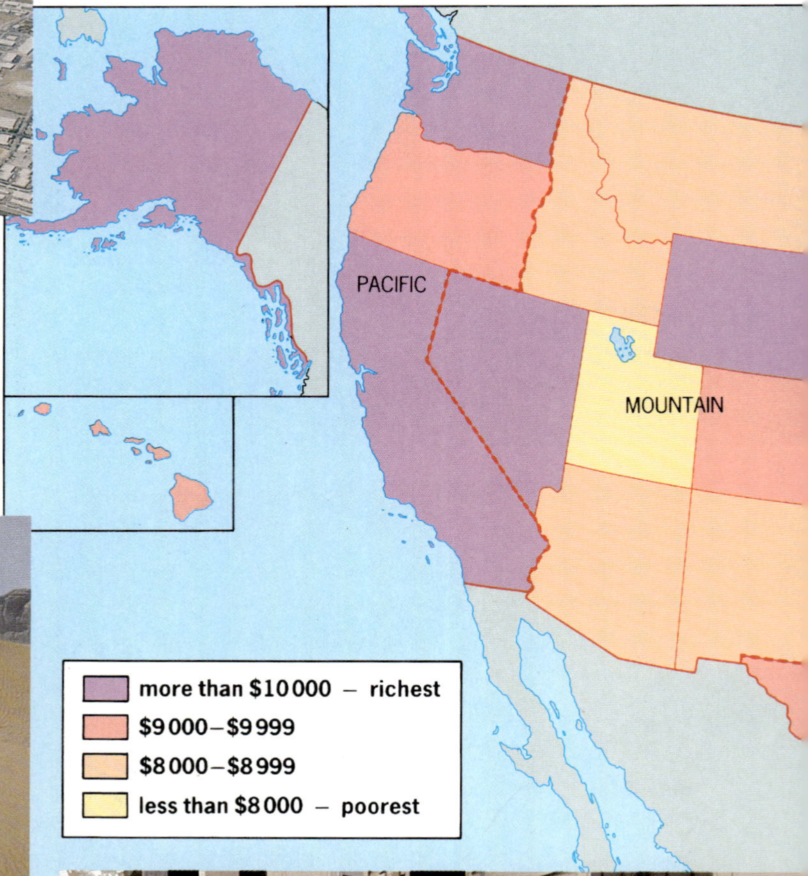

▲ CALIFORNIA

Hi-tech industry: microchips, aerospace, armaments
Rapid population growth in 1960s and 1970s
Mediterranean climate + irrigation = citrus fruit, vines
High standard of living for most
Legal and illegal immigrants from Mexico and Central America provide cheap labour

▲ THE NAVAHO NATION, ARIZONA

1.5 million Native Americans live in the USA
The Navaho people are the largest remaining group
Sheep herding and crafts provide a low income
Restricted to reservations; most land lost
High unemployment (40 per cent) and depopulation

➤ NEW ENGLAND

Farming, fishing and forestry since 17th century
New industry, finance and research, e.g. Boston
Population growth – movement from New York area
High standard of living

Quality of life in the USA depends partly on who you are and where you live (A). In any state there are variations in income. Even in the wealthiest states, inner city areas tend to be very poor and are usually inhabited by **minority groups**.

▲ APPALACHIA

Poor mountainous area damaged by mining and forestry
Low incomes, high unemployment
Poor white farmers
Low levels of education and skills
Tennessee Valley Authority (1933) and Appalachian Regional Development Act (1965) combat poverty

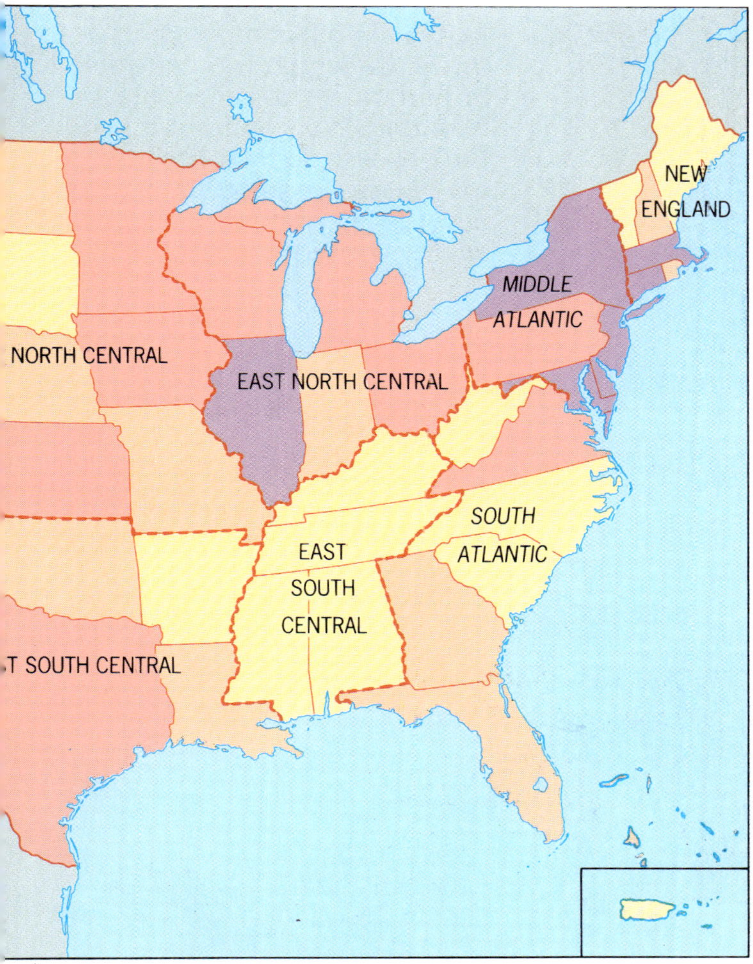

▲ **A** ***Income per person in the USA, 1980***

◀ ALABAMA

New Sunbelt industries in cities, e.g. Birmingham
Many poor Black people in farming
Low wages, high unemployment
High infant mortality, low life expectancy
Movement to cities of Alabama and rest of USA

1 The 'American Dream' is a rich, independent lifestyle. Which people in the USA might find it difficult to realize this dream?

2 **a** How do many Navaho people make a living?
b What jobs do other minority groups tend to get?

3 Compare one of the richer areas (California or New England) with one of the poorer ones. Try to explain this difference.

4 Describe the distribution of richer and poorer states in the USA (A). Use an atlas to name these states. Suggest why certain areas are poorer than others.

Energy in Japan

Japan is a highly developed and industrialized country which uses energy in many ways (A). Oil is the most important source (B). Japan has very few energy supplies of its own; 82 per cent of **primary energy** is imported (C, D).

Before 1950 Japan relied on its own coal, which was considered so important it was called 'black diamonds'. Cheap imported oil took over from this. However, the **oil crises** (E) caused Japan to develop alternatives to oil and energy conservation measures.

A *Energy is used in a variety of ways in Japan*

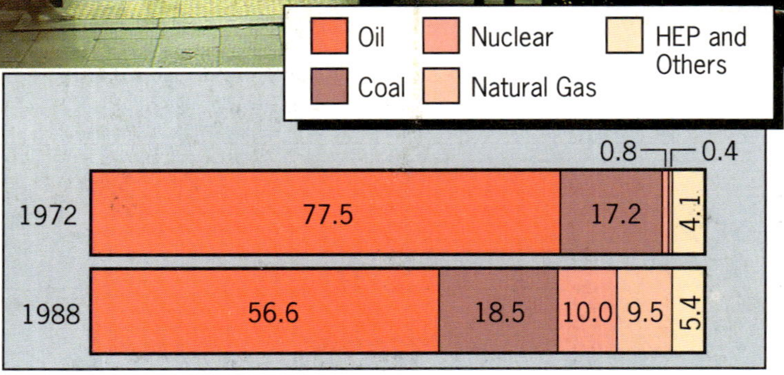

B *Sources of energy in Japan*

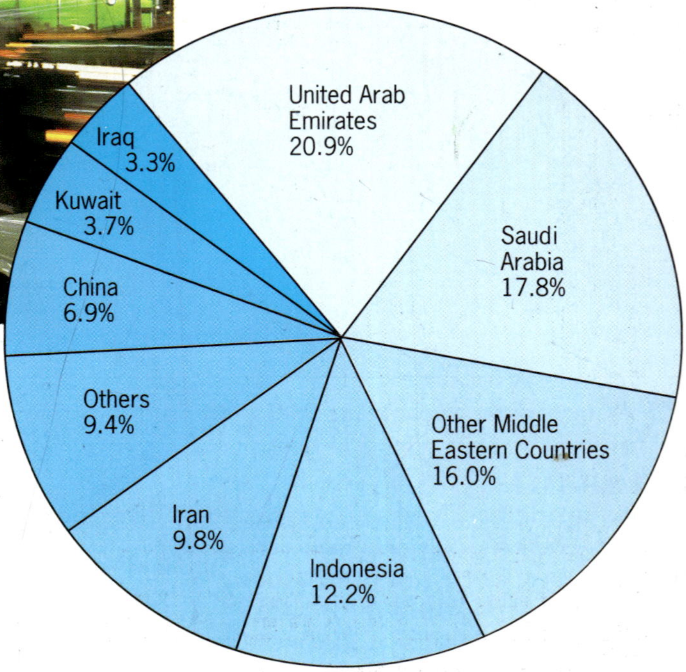

C *Where does the oil come from, 1990?*

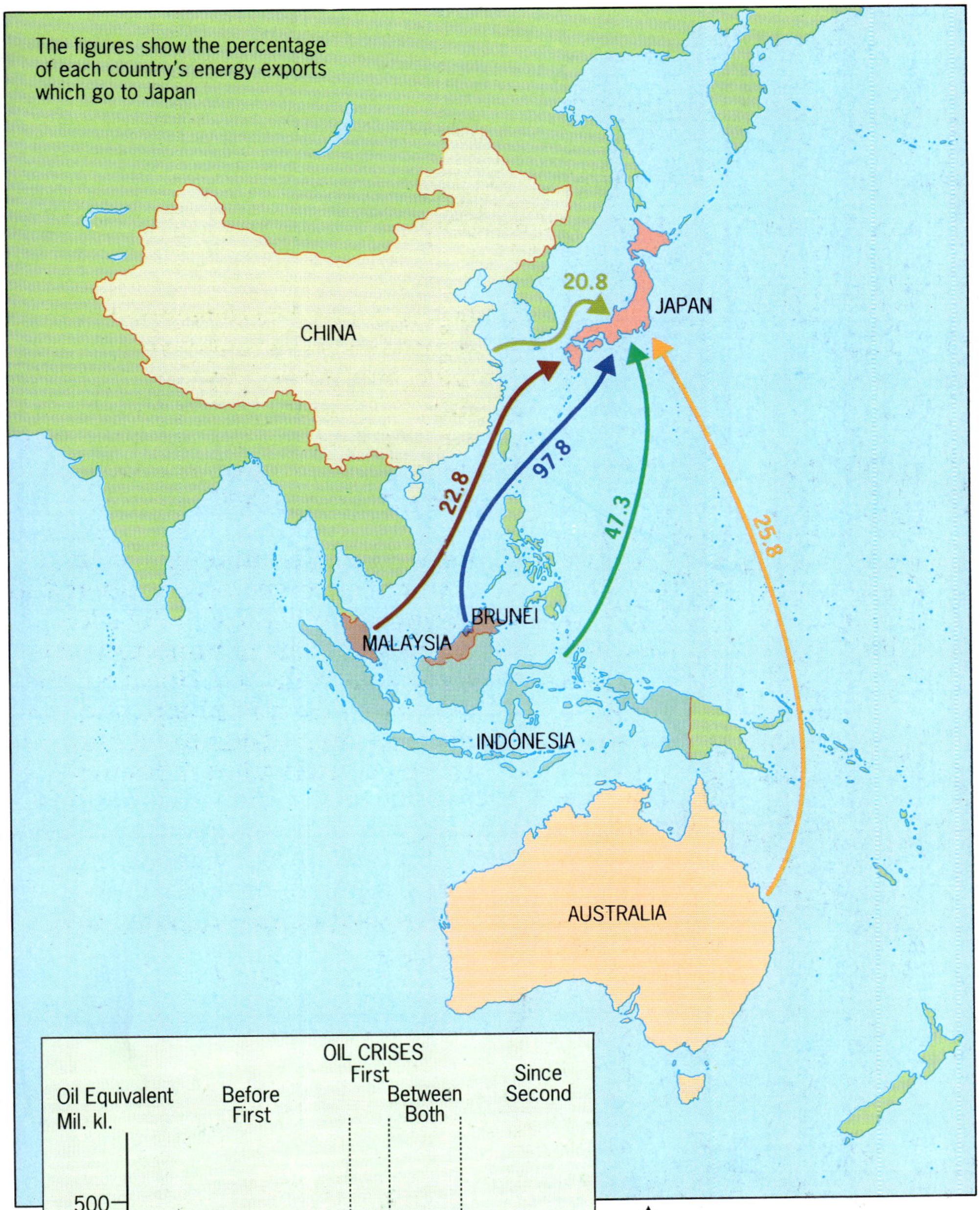

D ***The importance to other countries of trading in energy with Japan (1988 figures)***

1 Make a list of how energy is being used in A. Add to it other users that are likely to be found in a modern society like Japan.

2 **a** Describe the changes in the sources of energy between 1972 and 1988 (B).
b Suggest why these changes have taken place.

3 Look carefully at D and E.
a Which country is most dependant on selling energy to Japan?
b What effect might this have on that country?
c What are the difficulties for Japan in importing most of its energy supplies?

4 **a** Use the figures in F to draw a line graph showing people in favour of and against nuclear power in Japan.
b Describe what has happened to public opinion.
c Study graph E carefully. How does nuclear energy help in meeting demand? How may public opinion on nuclear energy affect Japan's energy policy in the future?

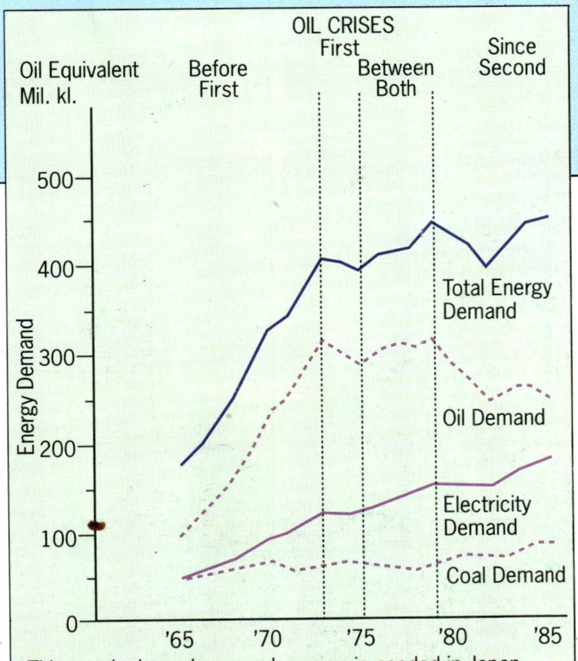

This graph shows how much energy is needed in Japan. It also shows how much is used of the three main sources.

E ***Changes in energy demand, Japan***

Year	For	Against
1978	55	23
1979	62	21
1980	56	25
1981	55	29
1982	52	30
1983	49	31
1984	47	32
1985	39	39
1986	34	41
1987	31	43
1988	29	46

F ***How the Japanese public view nuclear energy (%)***

Made in Japan

A ***The location of industrial regions in Japan***

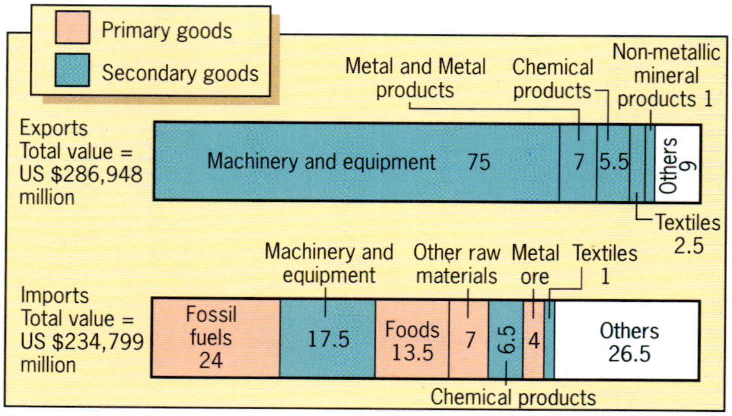

B ***Japan's trade, 1990 (%)***

Japan is one of the world's major industrial nations. It is a leading manufacturer of heavy goods such as steel and cars (E) and high technology goods, e.g. computers and electrical equipment (F, G). One reason for Japan's success is that its industries are modern and efficient.

Type of manufacturing	% of total workforce
Food, drink and tobacco	7
Textile goods	10
Forestry products	12
Construction and ceramics	5
Chemicals and chemical products	9
Metal refining	6
Engineering and metal products	49
Others	2

C ***Jobs in manufacturing, Japan (1989)***

D ***Industrial landscape, Tokyo Harbour***

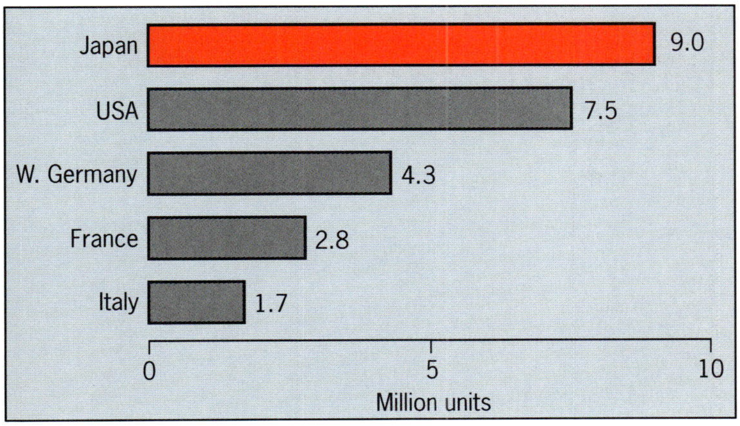

E ***International comparison of car production, 1990***

F ***International comparison of TV set production, 1990***

Country	No. of TV sets (millions)
China	14.6
Japan	13.9
USA	12.3
S. Korea	11.3

1 **a** On an outline map of Japan draw in the high ground using map G on page 4.
b Add the industrial regions from map A.
c Explain what this tells you about where industry is found in Japan.
d Suggest another reason which helps explain the location of the industrial regions in Japan.

2 **a** Use the figures in C to draw a bar graph.
b Describe what this tells you about jobs in manufacturing.

3 **a** Make a copy of the table below and list the products you can see in G.

Products	Name of companies

b Add any more you know of.
c Find out the names of the Japanese companies that make each product and add them to your table.

G ***Made in Japan: electrical goods***

Making steel in Japan

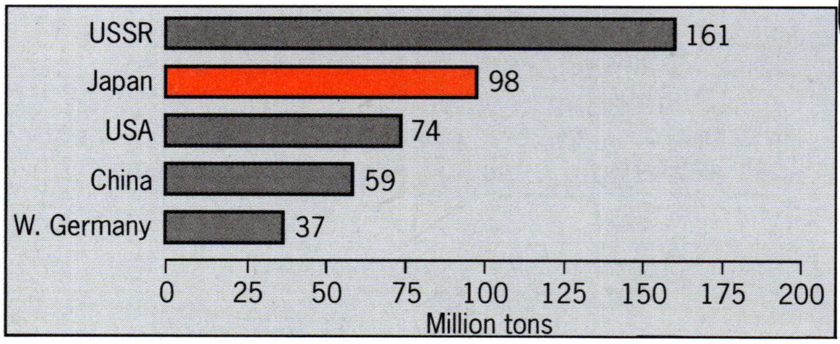

A ***International comparison of steel production, 1990***

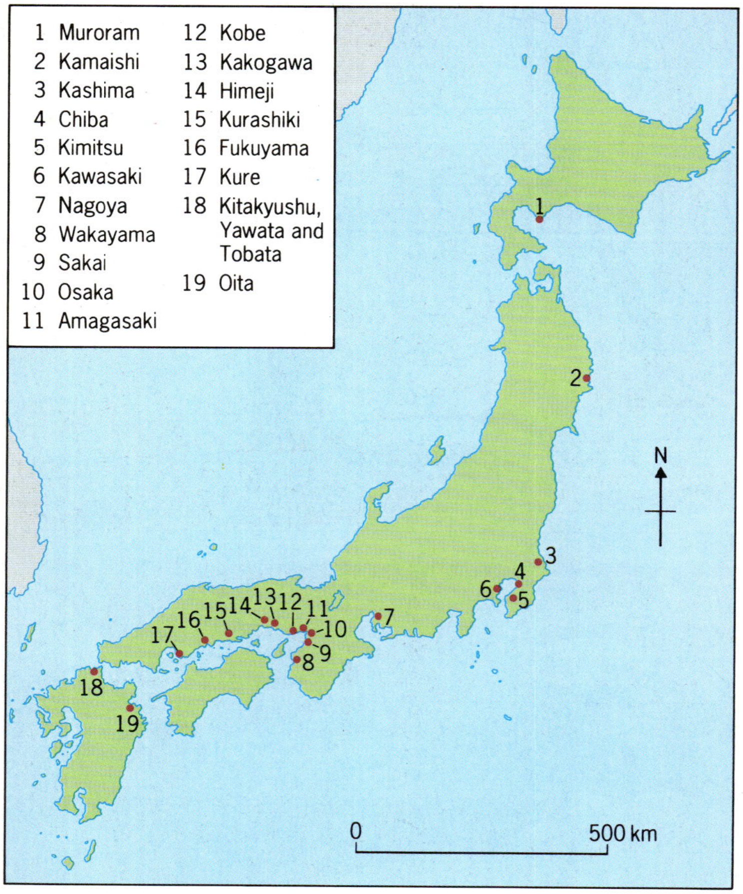

B ***Location of steelworks, Japan***

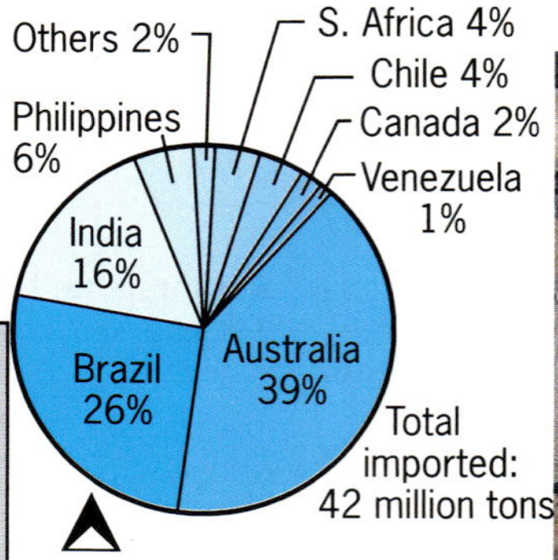

C ***Sources of iron ore***

D ***Iron ore mine, Western Australia***

E ***Iron ore carrier, Hammersley Harbour, Western Australia***

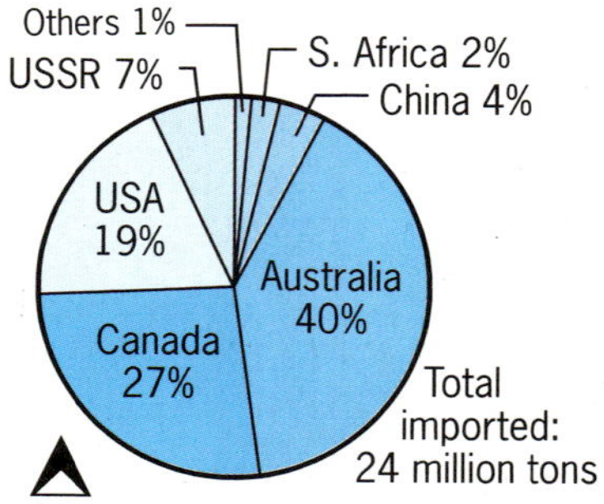

F ***Sources of coal***

G ***Brown coal mine, Victoria, Australia***

Japan's steel industry has been very important for a long time (A, B). It has provided the basis for two other major industries – shipbuilding and car manufacturing – as well as being used to produce many other goods (H, I). Steel is made cheaply because of modern and efficient works (J, K).

Steel production dropped slightly in the 1980s but has risen again recently. The Nippon Steel Corporation is the largest steel company in the world and makes a third of Japanese steel.

H ***Nanboko Bisan Seto Ohashi suspension bridge, from Yoshima***

I ***Skyscrapers, Tokyo***

J ***The steelworks outside . . .***

K ***. . . and inside***

1 **a** Trace map B and then use A on page 26 to name those steelworks not in the major industrial areas.

b Suggest why most are found in the same areas as other industries.

2 The location of steelworks is affected by a number of factors.

a The table below gives three of these factors. Use the information from this unit to fill in the evidence that these three are important for Japanese steelworks.

Raw materials	Site	Market

b Suggest other locational factors that may be important to the steelworks.

Changes in steel-making

19th century:	Small fishing village
1850s:	Discovery of iron ore in hills to the west
1857:	Blast furnace opened
1903:	Steel works built
1945–early 1970s	Steel works modernized – becomes one of the main centres of the Japanese steel industry
late 1970s:	Recession in Japanese and world markets for steel
1978:	Large-shape steel mill and one coke oven closed Workforce = 2972
1985:	One of two blast furnaces shut down Workforce = 2528
1988:	Decision taken to shut down remaining blast furnace and converters Workforce = 2300
1991:	Wire rod mill left and Kamaishi leading producer of high-quality wire for radial tyres Workforce in wire mill = 800 Workforce in new ventures = 1100

A ***A time-line of Kamaishi, a steel town***

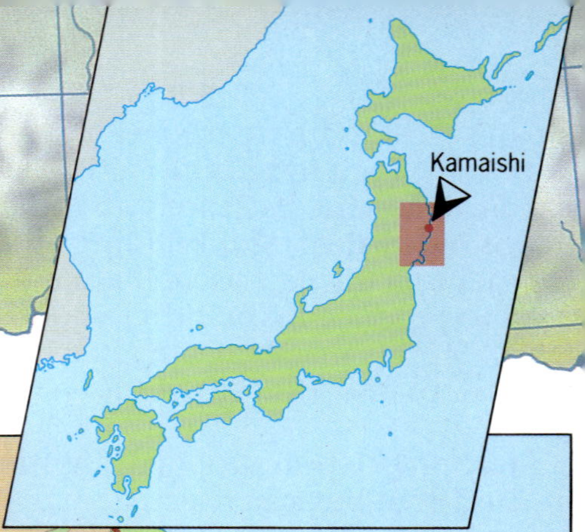

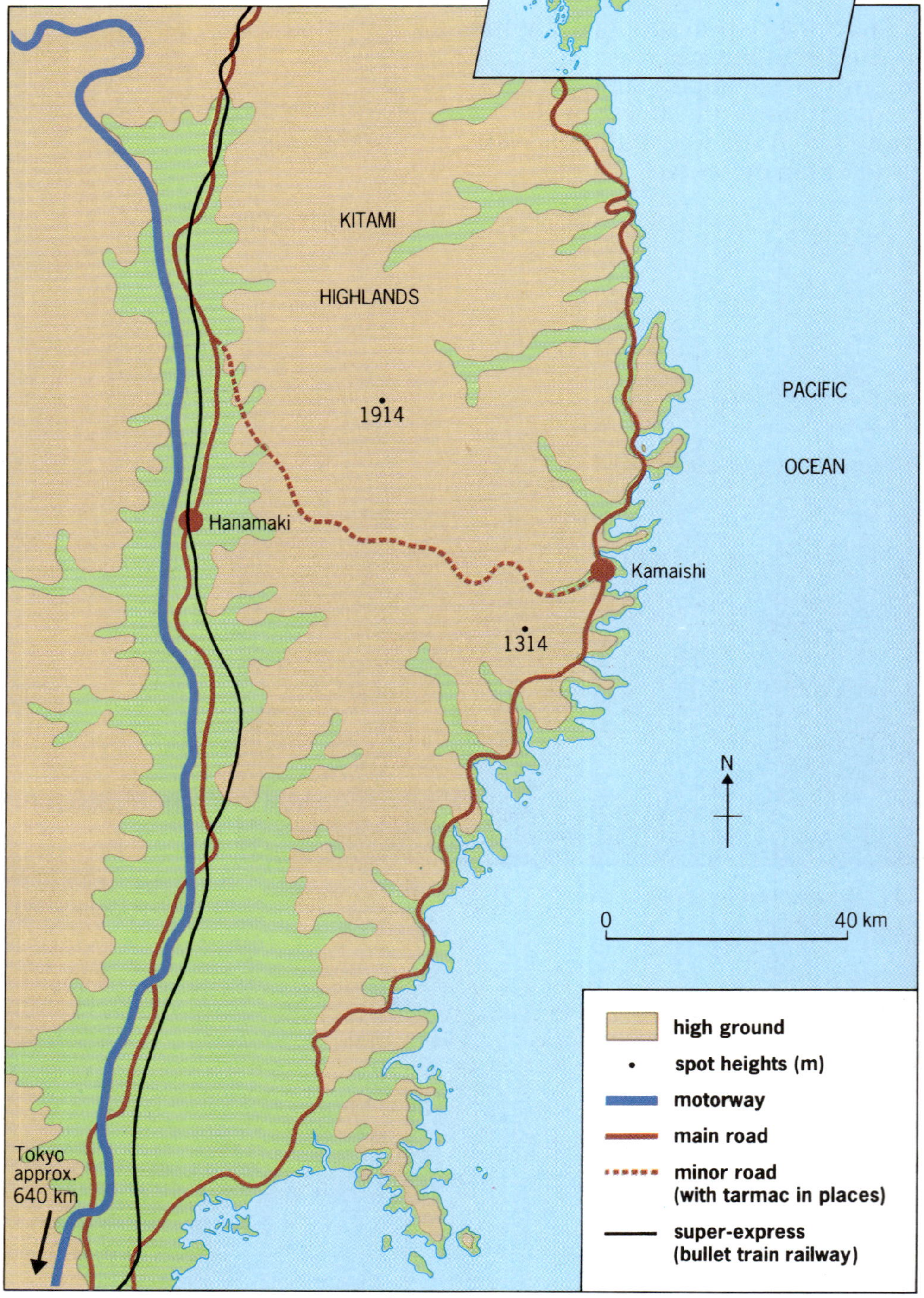

B ***The position of Kamaishi***

C ***A Nippon Steel factory***

D ***Changes in Kamaishi***

NEW DIRECTION FOR STEEL COMPANY

The Nippon Steel Corporation has launched its first computer this week. It's a small 'notebook' PC which will be made in Japan but sold in Europe. The reason for this move away from steel products was explained by a Nippon Steel spokesperson: "The world steel industries are having problems and so we have started to develop new products. We feel these small PCs are going to be important in the future and we shall become specialists. We already have a wide experience of computers in our steelworks."

E ***Future plans***

1 **a** Use the figures from A to draw a bar chart showing how the workforce has changed.
b Describe what this tells you about the workforce.
c In your own words explain why this has happened.

2 Read D carefully.
a Find Nagoya on map B on page 28. How far is it from Kamaishi?
b Imagine you are a steelworker at Kamaishi and the company has offered you a job at Nagoya. What would you feel about this?
c What is happening to Kamaishi as a result of the steelworks closing?

3 **a** Using all the information from this page and from pages 28–29 explain why the steel company prefers to develop business in places other than Kamaishi.
b Why have Nippon Steel decided to produce computers?
c Is this a good idea? Give reasons for your answer.

Environmental problems in Japan

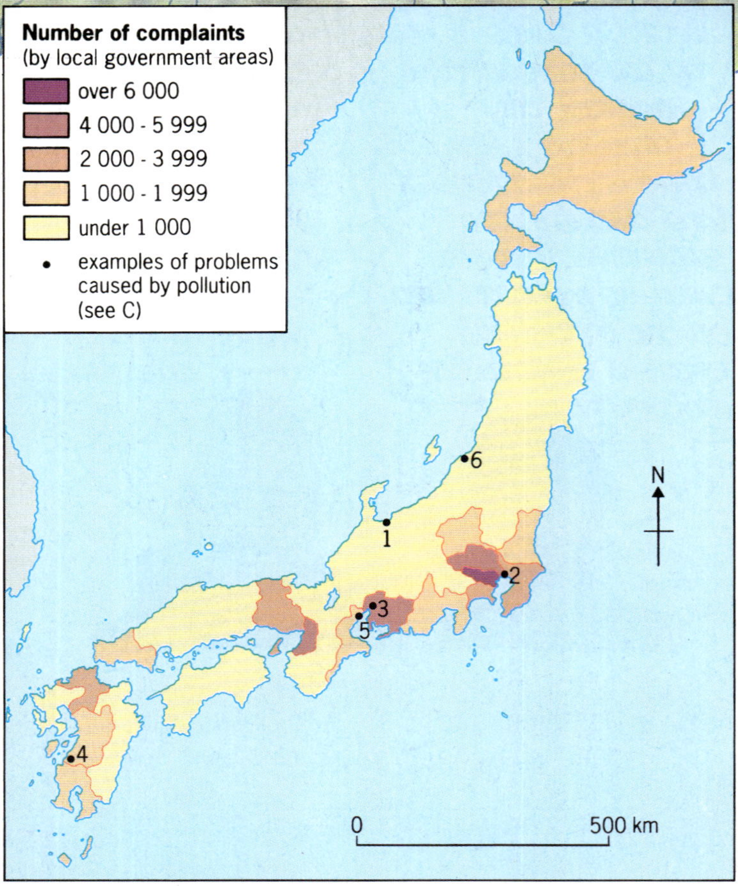

A ***Complaints about pollution***

B ***Air pollution indicators, Tokyo***

Where and when	Problem	Source	Effects
1 Toyama Began in 1945	River water polluted by cadmium. Fish and water-life poisoned. Drinking water affected.	Waste from lead and cadmium mine	People drinking the water suffered from itai-itai, a painful disease causing brittle bones. By 1980, 140 people had the disease and 81 had died.
2 Tsuruga 1981	Radioactive water flowed into sea	Nuclear power station	56 people exposed to radiation
3 Nagoya 1972	Air polluted by chemical fumes	Chemical and engineering companies	1 500 people treated in hospital
4 Minamata Began in 1953	Water polluted, fish and other sea-life poisoned by mercury	Chemical factory dumped mercury waste into sea	Minamata disease – loss of speech, sight, hearing, feeling in hands, etc. – affected 5 400 people. Many died.
5 Yokkaichi Began in 1955	Air polluted by chemical fumes	Petro-chemical refinery	Thousands of people suffered from asthma
6 Niigata Began in 1965	River water polluted by mercury. Fish and water-life poisoned. Drinking water affected.	Chemical factory dumped mercury waste into Agana river	By 1980, 900 people suffered from Minamata disease. 55 had died.

C ***Examples of problems caused by pollution***

Industry in Japan has been the cause of serious pollution problems. There are three reasons for this:

- industrial growth was very fast
- industries are concentrated in a number of areas
- until recently people were unaware of the dangers.

During the 1960s some companies were taken to court because they were causing ill health and sometimes death to people around them (A, B, C).

In 1971 the National Environment Agency was formed to tackle pollution problems. Now Japan spends more on anti-pollution measures than any other country in the world (D, E). Companies and ordinary people are now much more concerned (F).

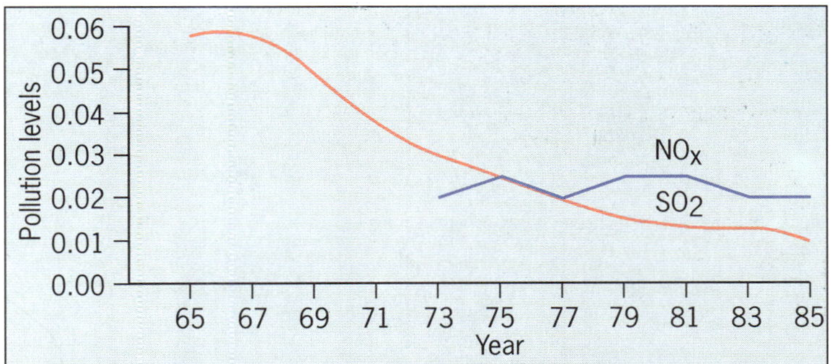

Nitrogen oxides (NO_x) and sulphur dioxide (SO_2) are both produced by the burning of fossil fuels (power stations, industries and vehicle exhausts)

D ***Air pollution, Japan***

Some measures introduced by the Japanese government to reduce air pollution

- reduction of import duties on low-sulphur oil
- financial support for the installation of **flue-gas desulphurization** technology
- incentives for industry to use less energy
- fines for industries producing a lot of pollution (the 'polluter pays' principle)
- introduction of smoke-free zones
- restriction of the amount of NOx produced by car exhausts (catalytic converters built into all new cars after 1975)

E ***How Japan reduced its air pollution***

F ***Some of today's environmental issues***

Issues of today	Environmental impact
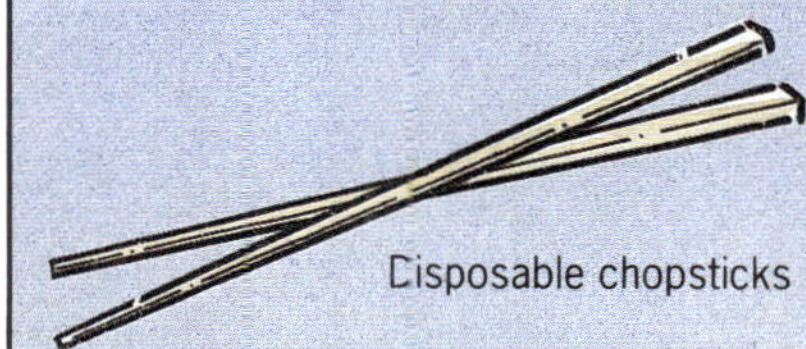 Disposable chopsticks	Unnecessary use of hardwoods from tropical rainforests. Disposal of waste.
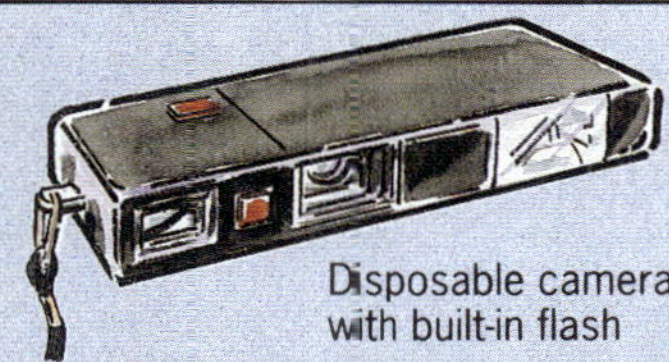 Disposable cameras with built-in flash	Waste of non-renewable resources. Chemical pollution from discarded batteries. Non-biodegradeable waste from batteries and casing.
 Cans with separate ring-pulls	Damage to wildlife Litter

1 Turn to page 26 and trace map A. Lay your tracing over A in this unit. What does this tell you about where pollution is found?

2 Study the information about what action was required to tackle air pollution (E). Write a report for the British government which outlines:

a what Japan has done to deal with air pollution

b how successful the measures have been (D).

c Recommend three of the measures in E to be adopted in Britain.

(You could get further information, about the measures and whether they've already been adopted in Britain, from the CEGB, Friends of the Earth, Greenpeace and the Environmental Health department of your local council.)

3 **a** Study F and decide what could be done to tackle the problems associated with each issue.

b Choose *one* of the issues and plan a publicity campaign to make people more aware of it. Give ideas on what they could do to help deal with it. Include leaflets, posters and badges.

Regional differences in Japan

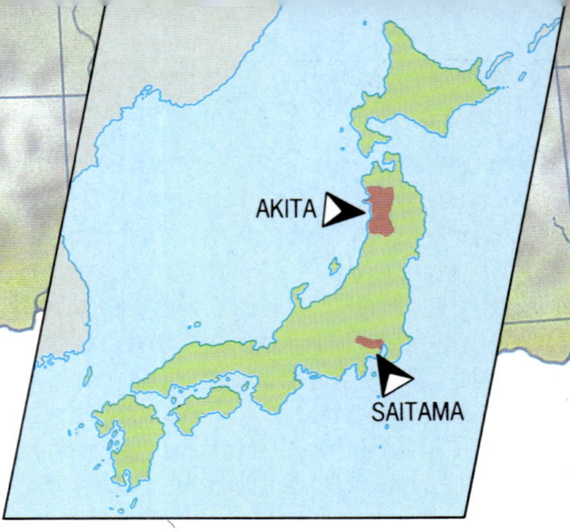

A

B

1 Study C – H carefully.
a Match up the photos A and B with the appropriate region. Give reasons for your choice.
b Describe the differences between the two prefectures. Use the following headings: Population (size and density), Wealth, Employment, Transport networks and Landscape.
c How do these factors help explain the differences in population, wealth and employment? (Consider distance from Tokyo, accessibility and relief.)

2 For each of the following say which of the two prefectures would be preferred:
a an industry looking for a site for a new factory
b a group of tourists visiting Japan for the first time
c a young person looking for a job.

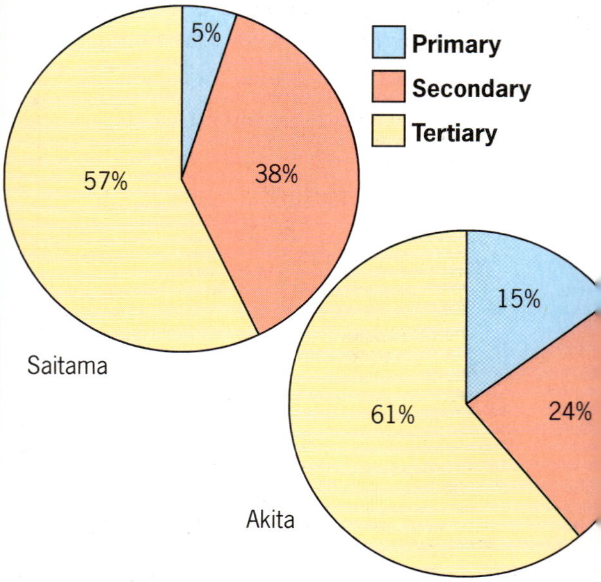

C ***Employment structures***

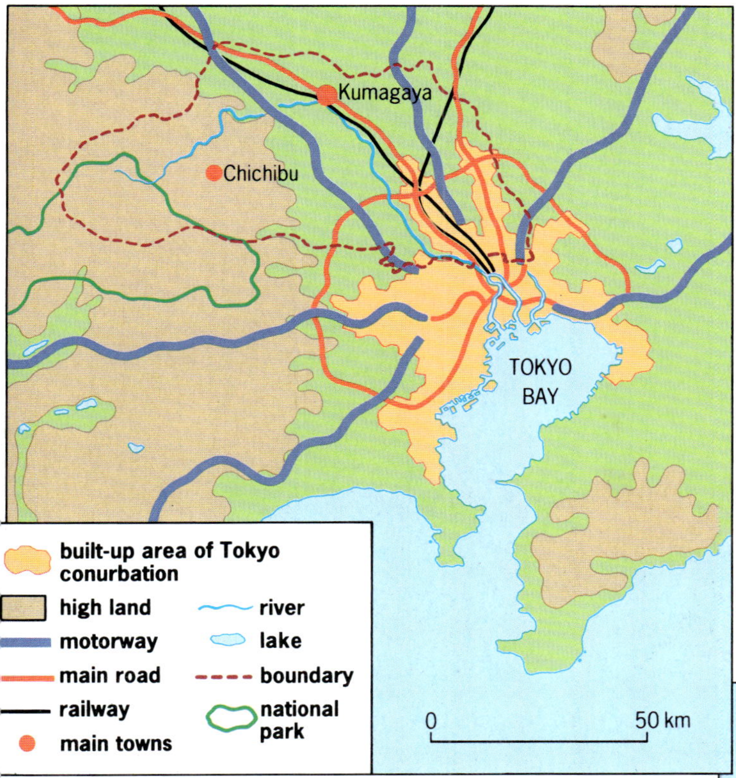

D ***Saitama prefecture***

- vegetables, plants and flowers grown for city population
- Fifth most important manufacturing area in Japan
- recent increase in supermarkets and department stores
- contains a special botanical garden and a park famous for its cherry blossoms

E ***Factfile on Saitama***

	Saitama	Akita
Distance from Tokyo	25 km	445 km
Population	5 863 678	1 254 032
Value of production (mill. yen)	12 689 006	2 678 116
Av. income per head (thou. yen)	2 333	1 837
Area (sq. km)	3 799	11 612

F ***Statistics for two prefectures*: Saitama and Akita (*a prefecture is similar to a county in Britain)***

- one of Japan's top rice-growing areas
- 71 per cent of region is forested
- one of few places in Japan where oil and gas are found
- most shops are small: 79 per cent employ less than four people
- skiing is available all year

G ***Factfile on Akita***

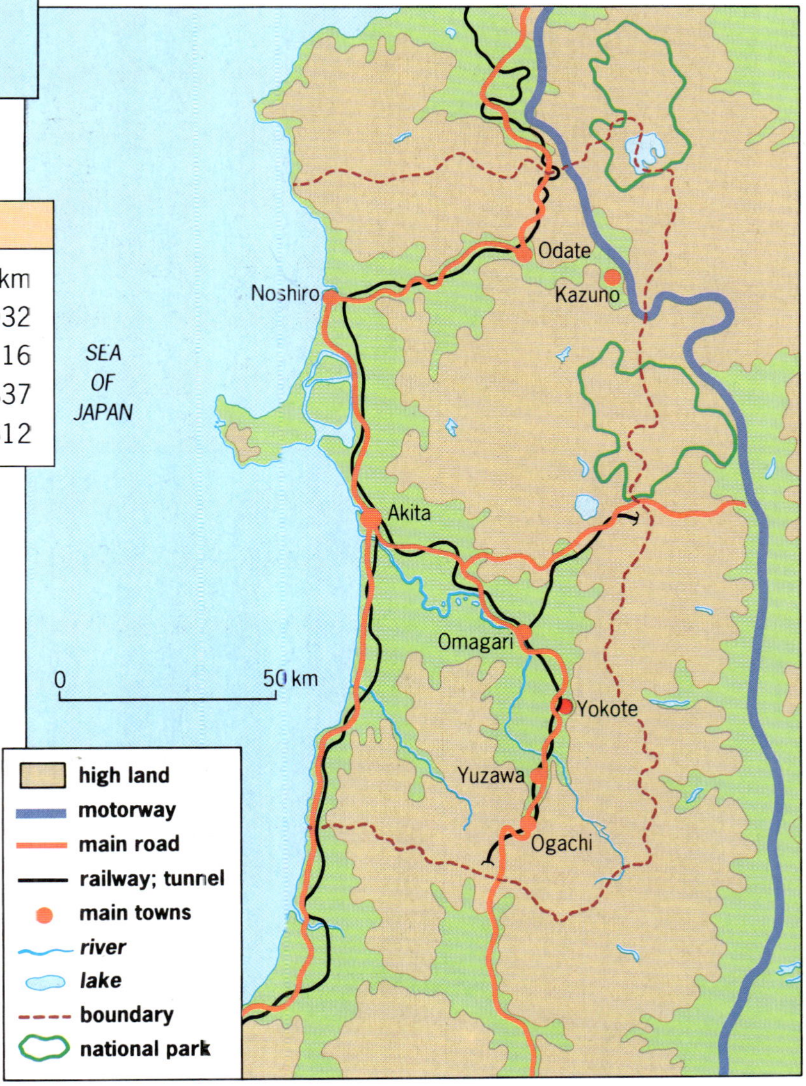

H ***Akita prefecture***

Energy in the USSR

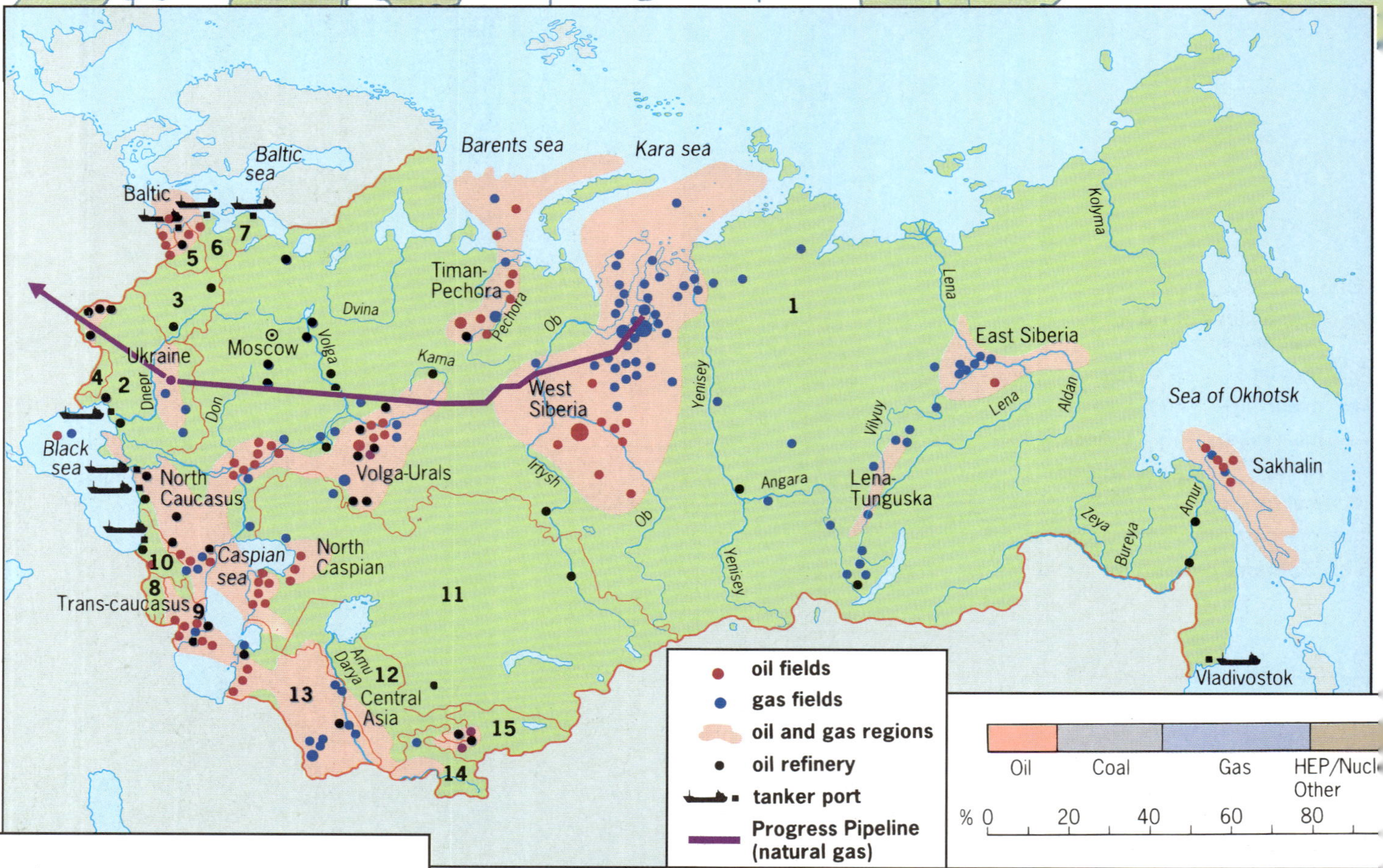

A ***Oil and gas in the USSR***

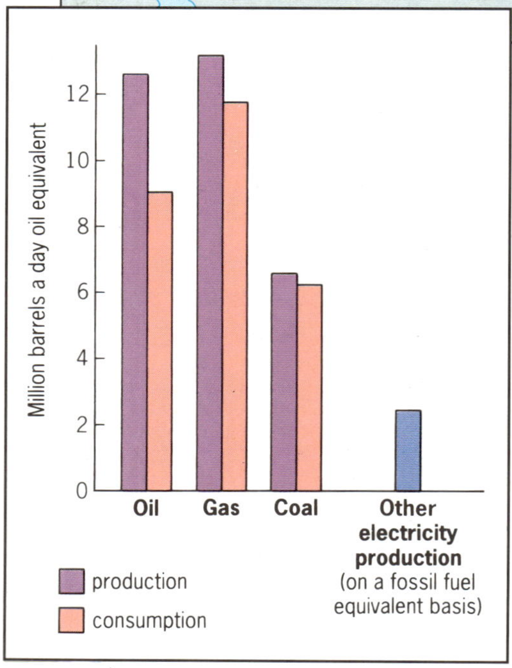

B ***Energy production and consumption in the USSR, 1988***

C ***Baku oil rigs in the Caspian Sea***

The former USSR is the world's leading producer of oil and gas. It is the third largest producer of coal. It has a large nuclear power capacity.

The USSR has some of the world's largest HEP (hydro-electric power) stations, many of them on the River Volga. The large Siberian rivers, the Ob and Yenisey, could produce more.

The former USSR exports much of its fuel. The Progress Pipeline was built in the 1980s to export natural gas from Siberia to East and West Europe.

Eastern European countries have received cheap fuel from the USSR in exchange for manufactured goods and political support. These policies are changing in the 1990s.

D ***Progress Pipeline, Siberia***

E ***The Kuzbas coalfield***

F ***HEP station on the Yenisei River***

1 Look at map A of oil and gas fields.
  a Describe the course of the Progress Pipeline. Use an atlas to help with the naming of mountain ranges, cities, rivers, etc.
  b How many oil refineries are there in the West Siberia oil and gas region? Where are most of the oil refineries? Can you explain this pattern?
  c Name the seas which have major tanker ports for exporting Soviet oil. Why are there none along the long northern coastline?

2 As communism gives way to a more open political and economic system in the Soviet Union and Eastern Europe, how will the pattern of Soviet fuel exports change? Is this likely to help the Soviet economy?

3 Graph B shows energy production and consumption in the USSR.
  a Calculate the difference between these two figures for oil, gas and coal.
  b What percentage is this for each fuel?
  c What do you think happens to the surplus oil, gas and coal produced?

Made in the USSR

A ***Major industrial regions in the republics of the former USSR***

'After the revolution in 1917 our communist rulers turned the country into a major industrial and military power. Our industries concentrated on machinery for agriculture and transport, and arms for the Red Army. Cement factories were needed for massive engineering projects such as hydro-electric power stations. The workers have all had jobs but there have been few goods for us to buy.'

B ***The USSR is trying to change the emphasis from heavy industry to consumer goods***

'We were happy working for the Revolution and put up with great hardship during World War II. After the war we expected our lives to improve. We wanted washing machines, TVs, fridges, cars, fashionable clothes and a variety of foods. There have always been shortages of these. President Gorbachev's policy of Perestroika promised us more of these consumer goods but we are still waiting to see them.'

C ***Minsk tractor factory***

As industry has grown in the USSR the types of job people do have changed. Many people left the countryside as farming was mechanized and jobs in heavy industry became available. These factory jobs are in the large cities. As the cities have grown there is more need for shop and office workers.

D ***Output of consumer goods, USSR, 1980–6***

	1980	1985	1986
ars (million)	1.3	1.3	1.3
elevision sets (million)	7.5	9.4	9.4
adio sets (million)	8.5	8.8	8.9
efrigerators and freezers (million)	5.9	5.9	5.9
ootwear (million pairs)	743.0	788.0	801.0
ashing machines (million)	3.8	5.1	5.4
abrics of all types (thousand illion sq m)	10.7	12.1	12.3
urniture (thousand million roubles)	5.3	7.5	8.3

	1980	1986	1987 (plan)
Electricity (thousand million kW/h)	1 294	1 599	1 665
Oil, including gas condensate (million tons)	603	615	617
Natural gas (thousand million cu m)	435	686	712
Coal (million tons)	716	751	744
Steel (million tons)	148	161	161
Iron ore (million tons)	245	250	247
Pig iron (million tons)	107	114	112
Tractors (thousand)	555	595	601
Paper (thousand tons)	5 288	6 156	6 435
Fabrics of all types (million sq m)	10 746	12 313	12 733
Footwear (million pairs)	743	801	816

E ***Output of basic industrial products, USSR, 1980–7***

1 **a** As the USSR built up its industry why do you think it concentrated on the types of goods shown in B?

b Why will it be difficult for the USSR to change from the manufacture of tanks and tractors to the manufacture of consumer goods? Think about skills, machinery, managers, finance, etc.

2 Look at map A. Select one industry. Describe its distribution, including which republics it is found in. Use atlas maps to compare the distribution of this industry with:

a centres of population

b sources of energy (oil, gas and coal)

c raw materials.

d Prepare a large and clear map to show your findings. It can then be displayed along with those of other students to create a picture of the main industries in the republics of the USSR.

3 Use statistics D and E to draw pictograms or bar charts to show how production is changing. If you work as a group you could cover all of these between you. Which goods seem to be increasing and which are static? Which goods to you think Soviet people would most like to see increased?

Russia and the Ukraine

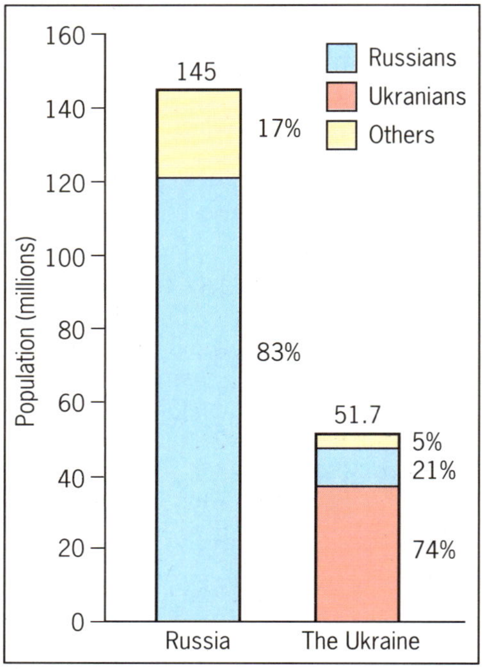

A ***Population structure in Russia and the Ukraine***

B ***Main industrial regions in the former USSR***

		Russia	The Ukraine
Gas output **Steel output** **Oil output**	} % of USSR total	78 58 91	2 35 1
Industrial output*		117	105
Urban population (% of total population each republic)		71	63
Average income (% above/below average Soviet wage)		+5.6	–8.4

*Based on 100 for USSR as a whole. Figures below 100 show less than national average; those above 100 show more than national average.

C ***Measures of development***

Russia

Russia was at the centre of the USSR from when the Union was established in 1922 until 1991. Present day Russia is self-sufficient in energy and food and is very rich in a variety of raw materials. It produces approximately 70 per cent of the USSR's agricultural and industrial output. However, agricultural and industrial activity varies greatly within the republic. The area east of the Urals – Siberia – is very rich in raw materials but, compared to the west, there is very little economic development.

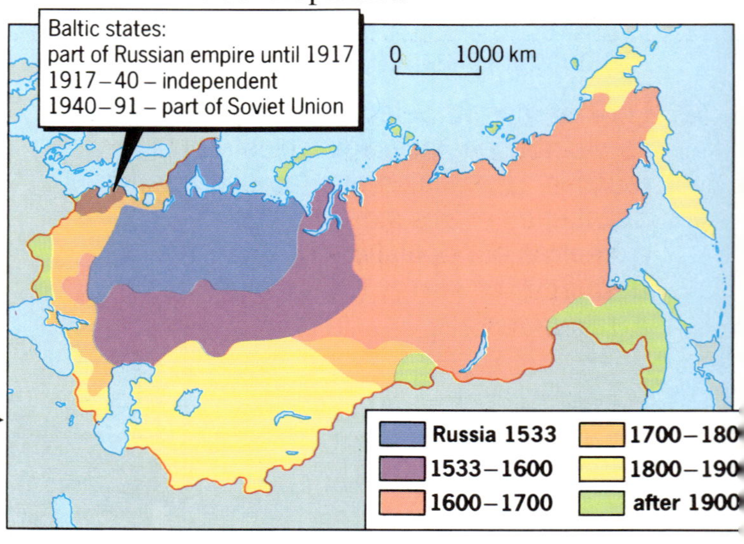

D ***Expansion of the Russian empire***

E *The attractions of Moscow . . .*

F *. . . and Siberia*

Moscow	J	F	M	A	M	J	J	A	S	O	N	D
Precipitation (mm)	39	38	36	37	53	58	88	71	58	45	47	54
Temperature (°C)	–13	–10	–4	6	13	16	18	17	12	6	–1	–7

G *Climate west of the Urals*

Yakutsk	J	F	M	A	M	J	J	A	S	O	N	D
Precipitation (mm)	4	2	3	4	5	6	4	7	4	5	3	4
Temperature (°C)	–50	–45	–32	–10	0	12	14	9	2	–15	–38	–48

H *Climate east of the Urals*

The Ukraine

This Republic is second to Russia in terms of resources and raw materials. It has many coal-fired and nuclear power stations (including Chernobyl). There is an important industrial area where steel, cars and consumer goods are made. Outside this area the land is used for agriculture and is particularly suitable for producing grain.

I *The Ukraine: trading links*

1 a Using all the information available explain why Russia can easily survive as an independent country. Include facts, figures, maps and graphs in your answer.

b Suggest reasons why Siberia has not become as developed and as populated as the west of Russia. Use G and H on this page, C on page 6 and an atlas to give a detailed answer.

2 The Ukraine has become independent. Some have said an independent Ukraine will not succeed.

a Work in pairs. One person is to prepare an argument for independence and one is to prepare an argument against. Use evidence to support your argument.

b Compare notes and decide which argument you find most convincing.

The Asian republics

A ***The Asian republics of the former USSR***

C ***Caucasu mountai***

B ***Measures of development***

	Georgia	Armenia	Azerbaijan	Kirghizia	Kazakh-stan	Turk-menistan	Uzbeki-stan	Tadz-hikistan
Industrial output*	65	78	56	50	65	49	45	41
Urban population (% of total pop. each republic)	53	67	54	39	56	48	42	34
Average income (% above/below av. Soviet wage)	–12.6	–5.6	–17.5	–14.7	–1.4	–1.1	–15.4	–17.5

*Based on 100 for USSR as a whole. Figures below 100 show less than national average; those above 100 show more than national average.

Trans-caucasia

The three small republics of Armenia, Azerbaijan and Georgia are separated from Russia by the high Caucasus mountains. The warmer climate here allows high value crops such as tea, tobacco and vines to be grown. The area is Russia's main source of these. The Baku oilfields in Azerbaijan are no longer a major source of fuel but this small republic is the main producer of oil-drilling machinery.

D *Tien Shan mountains*

E *Neryungri coal dressing plant*

Kazakhstan

Kazakhstan is the third major republic in the former USSR after Russia and the Ukraine. The huge coalfields of Karaganda and Ekibastuz provide fuel for the great steel and engineering industries of the Urals whilst Kazakhstan has its own large steelworks. The republic also produces large quantities of grain and meat from the extensive grasslands of the steppes. Many Russians have moved into Kazakhstan to work in its large cities. Today there are more Russians than Kazaks in the republic.

Central Asia

Uzbekistan, Kirghizia, Tadzhikistan and Turkmenistan make up the Central Asian republics. This area is one of the least developed parts of the USSR. There was some investment in agriculture so that the region could supply the USSR with grain, wool, cotton and meat. There were also massive irrigation schemes which were intended to extend agriculture into the desert areas. These schemes have caused great environmental damage to the Aral Sea. Industry has seen limited investment. The people in this area are amongst the poorest in the USSR.

F *Trade between the Asian republics and Russia*

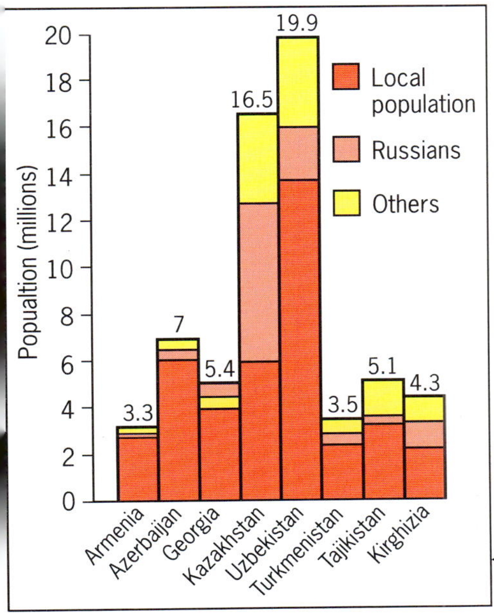

G *Population structure in the Asian republics*

1. Complete a copy of this table to show the exports and imports of the Asian republics.

	Exports	Imports
Primary goods		
Secondary goods		

2. Are the imports or exports of the Asian republics likely to be of most value?
3. There was little investment in the Asian republics during communist rule from Moscow. Food and raw materials were supplied to Russian cities and industries. How do you think this will affect the ability of the Asian republics to become independent states?

Gg 1/5d; Gg 2/7g, 8c; Gg 4/8c

The western republics

A ***The western republics***

B ***Measures of development***

		The Baltics Lithuania	Latvia	Estonia	Byelorussia	Moldavia
Gas output	% of USSR total	–	–	–	–	–
Steel output		–	–	–	3	–
Oil output		–	–	–	0.5	–
Industrial output*		107	141	135	86	64
Urban population (% of total population each republic)		64	70	71	59	42
Average income (% above/below average Soviet wage)		–0.7	+2.1	+12.6	–7.7	–17.5

*Based on 100 for USSR as a whole. Figures below 100 show less than national average; those above 100 show more than national average.

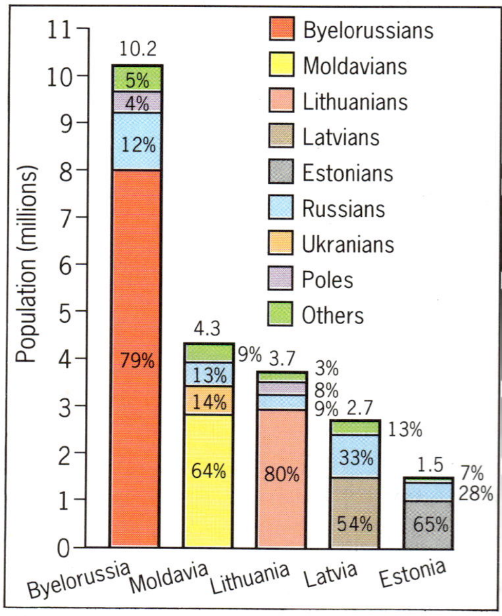

C ***Population structure in the western republics***

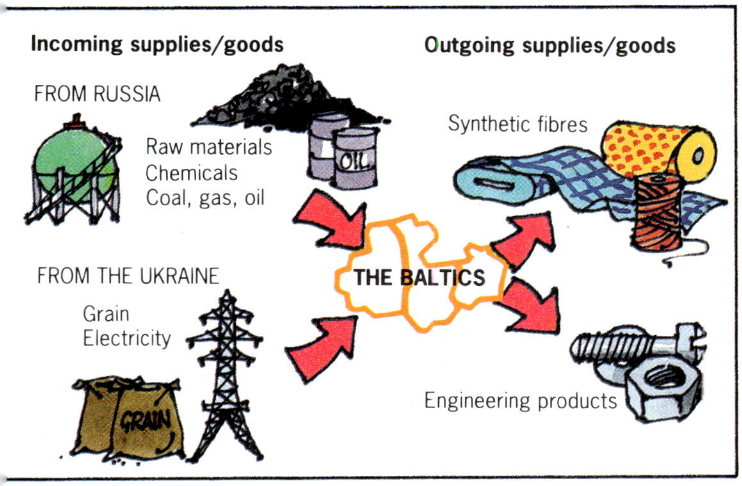

D ***The Baltics: trading links***

The Baltics – Estonia, Latvia and Lithuania

The Baltic states were part of the Russian empire until 1917 when they became independent. They remained so until 1940 when they were 'given' to the former USSR as part of the Nazi–Soviet non-aggression pact. Since the 1960s Russian workers have been encouraged by central government to move to these republics to work in centrally-controlled factories. The Baltic states have few resources so these have come from Russia too.

From 1940 onwards the Baltics have wanted to break away from the USSR. There were demonstrations in 1989, and independence was finally declared in 1991.

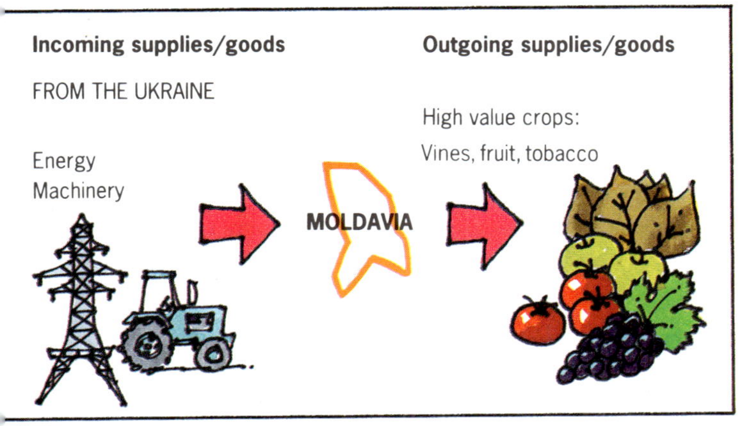

G ***Moldavia: trading links***

Moldavia

Moldavia is an important agricultural area. Some industry involving the processing of agricultural products has developed.

The majority of the population has closer links with the Romanians than with the Russians. They have recently become independent.

E ***Demonstration for independence for the Baltics***

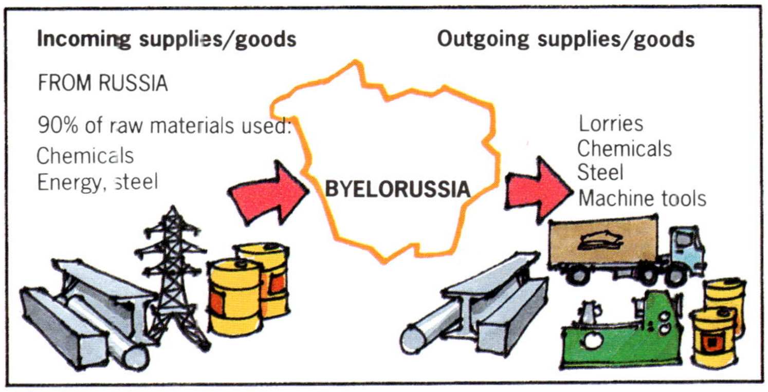

F ***Byelorussia: trading links***

Byelorussia

Byelorussia has few resources. However, the Soviet central government has encouraged industrial growth. So, using raw materials from Russia, this republic became the largest lorry manufacturer in the USSR, and is now independent. There are factories at Minsk and Vitebsk. There is also an important chemical factory.

1 Divide into groups of five. Each person takes one of the republics to research into. Use the information from these pages to suggest how each of the following may affect your chosen republic as it becomes independent:

- population diversity
- access to markets – within the USSR
  – outside the USSR
- resources (raw materials)
- industrial development
- social well-being

Present your findings to the group.
When everyone has reported back decide within your group which republic(s) will have
a least problems
b most problems
as they become independent.

Environmental problems in the USSR

The former USSR's old industries have caused some of the worst pollution in the world. All the places shown on the map suffer from environmental problems. This is a selection; there are others.

Until recently government and industries were not concerned about the environment. Nowadays, however, more and more people are becoming worried about the damage being done. The government is trying to control pollution by passing laws.

A – Kirishi

Cause Large chemical factory giving out poisonous fumes.

Effects Lung diseases have increased 35 times. Also, increase in deaths of babies.

B – Tbilisi

Cause Untreated waste from 200 industries entering river.

Effects Wildlife poisoned. Water unfit to drink.

C – Novokuznetsk

Cause Large steelworks, aluminium and engineering works polluting air and water.

Effects Acid rain. Wildlife poisoned. Increases in cancer and skin diseases.

A ***Environmental problems in the USSR***

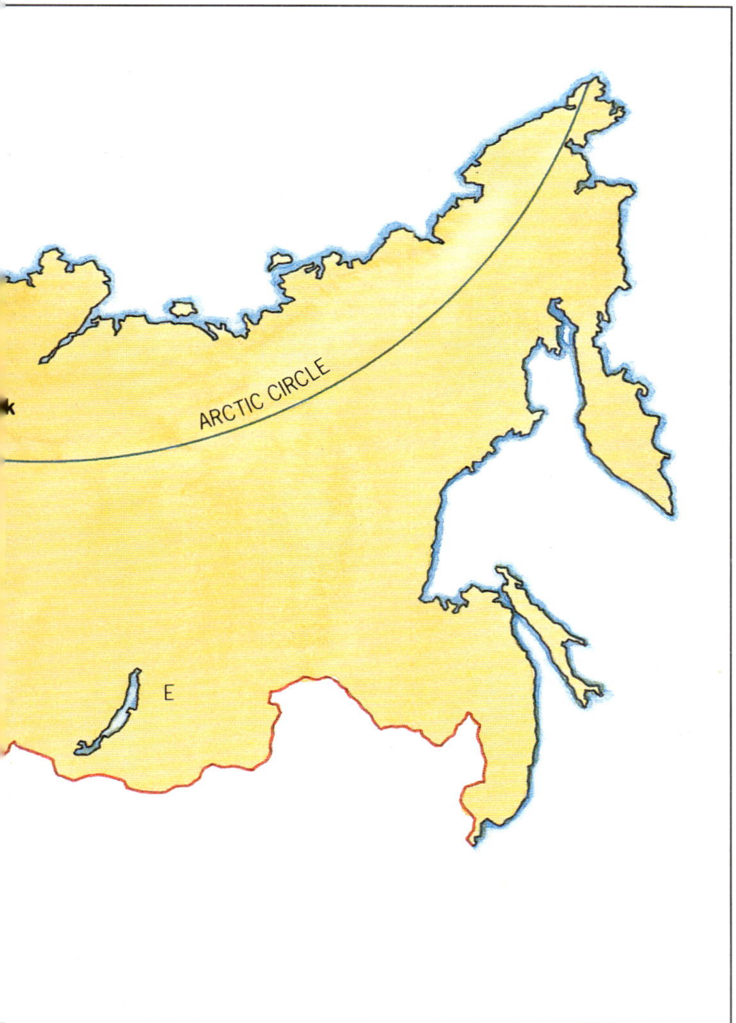

Work in groups. Imagine you are an environmental group in the USSR. Using information in this unit, design a campaign to make people more aware of the problems highlighted. You also need to persuade the government to take some action to improve the situation.

Here are some campaign suggestions:

- design badges, leaflets and posters
- write letters to newspapers
- write articles for newspapers and magazines
- prepare an item to be included in a TV or radio news programme.

D – Yamal Peninsula

Cause Oil and gas extraction. Building of pipelines and railways.

Effects Damage to plants and wildlife (destruction of habitats). People's lives disrupted.

E – Lake Baikal

Cause Two pulp and paper mills polluting water with waste products.

Effects Destruction of plants, poisoning of fish and animals.

Glossary

Acid rain Rain containing an unusual amount of acidity.
Capital Money used to pay for an industry.
Ecosystem The relationship between plants and animals within their environment or habitat.
Electronics Goods which are controlled by microchips.
Energy Power from renewable (e.g. solar) and non-renewable (e.g. coal) resources.
Flue-gas desulphurization Special technology fitted to chimneys which removes the sulphur dioxide (SO_2) from the smoke and fumes.
Free trade The import and export of goods without taxes or quotas.
Footloose An industry which can locate anywhere.
Fossil fuels Carbon-based fuels made up of the fossilised remains of organisms found in sedimentary rocks, e.g. coal, oil and gas.
GDP (Gross Domestic Product) The total value of all production and services in one country.
Heavy industry Manufacturing on a large scale of bulky products e.g. iron and steel, shipbuilding.
HEP (hydro-electric power) Power generated by using the force of moving water.
Hi-tech Advanced manufacturing or information services normally using very modern techniques and micro-chips.
Import barriers Methods for discouraging the importation of goods, e.g. by taxation or quotas.
Import duties Taxes charged on imported goods.
Information systems Microchip technology plus the people who make up an organization which uses that technology.
Manufactured goods Articles made by the conversion of raw materials, normally using machinery.
Market The demand for any good or service.
Migration The movement of people either within or between countries.
Minerals/mineral resources Substances obtained by mining, quarrying or drilling for industrial use.
Minority group An ethnic group which is less numerous than the dominant group of people in a country.
Multinational A company with interests in a number of different countries.
Natural resources Things from the natural world, such as wood and coal, that people use in a variety of ways.
Nuclear power Electrical power generated by nuclear reactions using uranium or plutonium.
Oil crises Times when the price of oil shot up, making it difficult to afford to buy it.
Oil shale A sedimentary rock containing oil.
Petro-chemicals Chemicals made by the conversion of crude oil.
Pharmaceuticals Drugs and medicines.
Pollutants Chemical or mineral by-products of industry which damage the environment.
Primary employment Jobs involved in farming, fishing mining etc. Involved in the production of raw materials.
Primary energy Energy, such as coal, gas and oil, which can also be used to produce electricity.
Protection The protection of a country's industry by imposing import duties (taxes) on goods which might compete with those of the home country.
Quaternary employment Jobs using information technology to provide services to people and industry.
Quota A maximum limit set on the amount of a good which may be produced or imported.
Refinery A large factory where crude oil is converted into a variety of products, including petrol and bitumen.
Republics A state ruled without a 'Royal Family', normally having a President as Head of State.
Reserves The quantity of a mineral resource left.
Secondary employment Jobs involved with the manufacture, processing or assembly of goods.
Semi-skilled An occupation requiring some training.
Skilled An occupation requiring a lot of training.
Solar power Power generated by using the heat energy of the sun.
Strip mining Mining by the removal of overlying soil and rocks in order to expose the mineral itself.
'Sunrise' industries Newly established hi-tech industries.
Superpowers Those small number of states which have unusually large economies and political influence.
Supertanker A very large ship used to transport crude oil.
Synthetic Usually textiles. Manufactured from petroleum products.
Tertiary employment Jobs involving the provision of a service to people, e.g. transport, health, retailing.
Trading nation Any country which is involved in importing and exporting goods.